Big Sky Ghosts

BIG SKY GHOSTS

EERIE TRUE TALES OF MONTANA

Volume Two

DEBRA D. MUNN

PRUETT PUBLISHING COMPANY
BOULDER, COLORADO

Printed in the United States
06 05 04 03 02 01 00   5 4 3

Library of Congress Cataloging-in-Publication Data

(Revised for vol. 2)

Munn, Debra D., 1953–
    Big sky ghosts.

    Includes bibliographical references and indexes.
    1. Ghosts—Montana. 2. Haunted houses—Montana. I. Title.
BF1472.U6M849   1993   133.1'09786   93-3176
ISBN 0-871-0808838-X (v. 1. pbk. : alk. paper)
ISBN 0-871-0808839-8 (v. 2. pbk. : alk. paper)

Book design by Jody Chapel, Cover to Cover Design

To Janell Hanson, a true friend and "kindred spirit."

Contents

Introduction

Montana may be one of our sparsest states as far as living, breathing inhabitants go, but it can certainly boast of more than its fair share of denizens from the world beyond. I reached this conclusion after spending three years interviewing over one hundred residents (of the earthly variety) and searching through books, newspapers, and files of historical associations. I found so many spooky stories, in fact, that *Big Sky Ghosts: Eerie True Tales of Montana* had to be divided into two volumes, the second of which you're holding in your hands.

I have tried to be as complete and as accurate as possible in reporting the stories, and, wherever I could, I have used the real names of those experiencing the phenomena. To protect those requesting anonymity and to keep from identifying the families of certain individuals now deceased, I have used pseudonyms, indicated as such in the text. Readers will find, both in this book and in Volume One, that the names and accounts of some interviewees appear in more than one chapter. As I explained in the first book, some people seem more prone to supernatural occurrences than others, just as some sites are more apt to absorb psychic impressions.

Contained in this book are tales to please all aficionados of the supernatural, but a word of caution may be in order. One reviewer of *Big Sky Ghosts,* Volume One, complained that its stories weren't "imaginative" enough, and though he undoubtedly meant this comment as negative criticism, I view it in a positive light. The author of a collection of supposedly "true" ghost stories has no right to "juice up" her material to make it read like a Stephen King novel—instead, she must record the facts as they are presented to her, even when they are less than sensational. And while true ghost stories have the power to mystify, enthrall, and even give us a bad case of the willies, they rarely horrify us in the way that their fictional counterparts do. Instead, true ghost stories both delight and threaten us because they challenge our complacent view of the world and they force us to realize that no matter how much we human beings have come to understand about the nature of reality, we still have a lot to learn. The universe is a much more mysterious place than we know. But don't take my word for it. Enter the world of *Big Sky Ghosts* and find out for yourself.

One
· · · · · ·

The Man in the Photograph

O ne of the leading theories about hauntings is that impressions of events that trigger strong emotions are somehow recorded on the physical environment: on the walls and floors of buildings or on objects in nature such as trees and stones. Then, according to this same theory, when the conditions are right, these same recorded impressions are somehow "replayed"—often to the horror of any living person unlucky enough to be present at the time.

If this theory is correct, we would all do well to check out the past history of any home we are thinking of buying or renting, and we might be especially wise not to move into any dwelling in which violence has occurred.

Emma Huntsman, known to friends as "Gidget," wasn't thinking of any such thing in the early 1970s when she decided to fix up the big white two-story house down the street from where she had been living in the southwest part of Great Falls.

"My landlord was selling the house where I was, and this other place, built around the turn of the century, was empty," Gidget explained. "I figured it could be a really nice home if it were cleaned up and all the old junk in it was thrown away. So the landlord and I made an agreement that I would tidy up the place in exchange for the first month's rent."

No sooner had Gidget and her two children, seven-year-old Tanya and five-year-old Doyle, begun the cleanup when a neighbor from next door came by to express her concern.

"'Are you going to move in here?' she asked, and when we said we were, she warned us, 'Well, there are some really weird things happening in this house.' Then she said that two women had died there and that the cause of death of one of them was uncertain. The woman had been found dead in the house, and although the coroner had apparently claimed that she died of natural causes, a lot of people seemed to think that her husband had murdered her, perhaps by strangling. And neighbors had sometimes heard the sounds of a woman crying inside the house when there was clearly no one there.

· · · · · ·
3

"I told the neighbor that I didn't believe in any such thing as a haunted house and that the speculation about the deaths was just hearsay, anyway. But the neighbor insisted again that some very odd things had happened there.

"The kids and I went ahead and cleaned the place up and then we moved in," Gidget continued. "While clearing out some junk from my son's bedroom upstairs, I discovered a door in the closet that led into an adjoining attic. The door fastened with a hook and eye, so I hooked it shut and told the kids to leave it that way and to stay out of the attic. It was an old house that had suffered some neglect, and I was afraid that they might hurt themselves by falling through the ceiling.

"Later, many times when I went upstairs I found the door to that attic open. I blamed the kids and threatened to punish them, but they always swore up and down that they weren't the ones who had unlocked it. This happened so often that one time I bent the hook around so that it couldn't be removed from the eye without using pliers. But even that didn't solve the problem, and we still found the door open from time to time.

"Another odd thing about that house was that a person could stand directly in front of the heater when it was on and still feel so much cold air that it was like being outdoors," Gidget recalled. "It was absolutely chilling! This cold wind seemed to blow through the house, and often when I told the kids to shut the door we found that it had been closed all the time."

In addition to breezes that came from nowhere and a door that wouldn't stay shut, the family was also troubled by an upstairs light that turned itself on in the wee hours.

"For a while, we didn't realize what was happening," Gidget said. "The upstairs was cold in the winter and the kids had become too scared to sleep up there anyway, so most of the time we all slept downstairs. One afternoon when I was outside, a neighbor asked if we were okay. I assured him that we were, and he told me that the reason for his concern was that he'd seen the bedroom light on upstairs at about two o'clock that morning and he wondered if anybody had been sick.

"I told him that he must have been mistaken, that we had all been asleep downstairs, and that, anyway, there would be no reason for anyone to turn on that light at such an ungodly hour. Then the neighbor just shrugged and said, 'Well, this isn't the first time I've seen it on in the middle of the night. I've seen it several different times, in fact.'"

During this period, Gidget was working at the NCO club at Malmstrom Air Force Base on weekend nights and attending school in the daytime. In one of her classes she had met a friend who eventually decided to move in with her.

"My son was sleeping with me most of the time, anyway," Gidget explained, "so Linda went ahead and moved into his room. One time she told me that she had experienced a strange sensation when she was up there, but I tried to reassure her that nothing was wrong and that she would be perfectly safe."

One night, however, Gidget arrived home from work to find her new friend downstairs, trying to sleep on a cot in the music room. "I asked her what she was doing down there and she told me in no uncertain terms, 'I'm not sleeping up there. There are weird things going on in that place. The floors squeak, the light comes on when there's noboby around, and that room just gives me the creeps.'

"I tried to reassure her again, to tell her that nothing was wrong," Gidget recalled. "I was standing in front of the heater, just starting to pull off my shirt to get ready for bed. And then I looked up just in time to see the upstairs light come on.

"I didn't see how she could have done it, but I asked her anyway: 'Linda, did you turn on that light upstairs?' And she said, 'No, I told you—there are some weird things happening up there.'

"Next I asked her where the kids were and she said that they had decided to sleep upstairs that night. Well, naturally, I figured that either Tanya or Doyle had turned on the light, but when I went up there to check, they were both sound asleep. I woke them up and made them go downstairs and get into bed with me.

"As we were lying there trying to get to sleep, we could all hear the old wooden ceiling creaking, just as if someone were walking back and forth up there on the floor of the bedroom. That made me even more nervous, so I got out of bed and went up to check to make sure nobody was there," Gidget said. "Of course, nobody was, so I went back to bed. But the creaking started once more, sounding just like somebody walking around. I was really scared this time so I called a friend who was an MP out at the base. The MP came over and checked the house and even made sure that there were no footprints in the snow leading to it. Then I locked and nailed shut the window to the attic so that there was no possible way for anyone to break in. But I don't see how anyone could have done that anyway, because three little wooden eaves across the porch would have prevented it."

Three or four weeks later, Gidget was sitting in the kitchen finishing a letter to her mother while waiting for her tub to fill up in the adjacent bathroom.

"Suddenly I felt some very cold air blowing in on me and I yelled to the kids to shut the door. They told me that it wasn't open, but I couldn't believe it. 'There's cold air blowing in here from somewhere,' I told them. 'Are you sure that door isn't open?' Then I walked into the bathroom and saw that the window had been removed from the frame—I mean it was completely off, sitting upright against the house as if someone had placed it there deliberately. If it had fallen, it wouldn't have landed like that. Fresh snow was all around and there were no footprints or any other signs that anyone had been there. And there were no footprints on the roof either.

"I hollered at the kids to check to see if someone was in the alley or if they could find any footprints in that direction. But the only footprints there were those of the kids themselves where they had walked out, and they hadn't gone anywhere near the bathroom window."

Eventually, Gidget began to connect the unexplained phenomena with a photograph that she had found in an old trunk in a shed behind the house. The subject of the picture was a man in his twenties or thirties, and he had apparently been married in turn to each of the two women who died in the house. Behind the photograph, Gidget had found a framed painting of a charming old homestead complete with a horse, milk wagon, and chickens set against a background of mountains and trees.

"The painting is beautiful and the scene looks like somewhere I'd like to live. In fact, the house itself, the chickens out front, almost everything in that painting, looks remarkably similar, almost eerily so, to where I live now in California. But the photograph of the man bothered me. When I looked at his eyes, he seemed to be looking right back. For a long time, everywhere I went I felt that this man was with me, and I began to wonder whether he was responsible for the weird things that were going on. So I hid the photograph behind the painting to get it out of my sight."

Even with the picture concealed, the eerie manifestations continued until everyone in the family decided they had had enough.

"We decided to move back to Florida," Gidget said, "and a friend of mine offered to help us save money by letting us stay at his place for a couple of weeks before we left the state. During this time, I still returned regularly to our house to pick up the mail.

"One day I had just gotten everything out of the mailbox and was getting into my car to leave when the man who was renting the place came out and said, 'Wait a minute—I want to ask you something. I know this sounds funny, but did weird things happen to your family when you lived in this house?' Then he went on to say that he had been forced to nail shut the upstairs closet door to the attic after a mysterious woman's voice kept calling for his younger son to come up the stairs. It was as if she were trying to entice him to go up there.

"In another incident, the man's wife laid her cigarette in an ashtray and when she picked it up again she couldn't understand why it was wet on both sides. Equally strange was the way that their sons' wads of chewing gum would reappear in the ashtray after having been thrown into the garbage. This new family didn't like living with ghosts any better than we did, and they decided to leave not long after I spoke with the man."

Gidget and her children moved to Florida and then to California and, fortunately, no ghostly presences followed them. Gidget returns to Montana from time to time, and whenever she's in Great Falls, curiosity prompts her to drive by her former home. Her most recent return was during Christmas 1991, and at that time the house looked deserted and the windows were boarded up.

And what became of the photograph of the man suspected of killing at least one of his wives?

"I thought I had thrown that picture away, until the back of the portrait came off and I found it there again," Gidget said. "Without realizing it, I had left it in storage with my stuff for almost a year in Florida, before I finally found a place to live. When I saw that man's face again, it gave me an eerie feeling, and I thought, 'This time, you'd better leave me alone!'"

Two
......

Virginia City, Ghost Capital of Montana

Professional parapsychologists should make a special trip to Virginia City, Montana, to study the psychic phenomena occurring there. The town was at one time the territorial capital, and it still seems to reign as the "ghost capital" of the state, with many of its year-round and summer residents claiming that there is indeed something very different about the place.

From its earliest days as a gold-mining mecca, Virginia City has had a reputation as a violent town—during a six-month period in 1863, 198 murders took place, averaging about one a day. Many of the killings were committed by Sheriff Henry Plummer and his gang, the Road Agents, and a number of these outlaws were themselves hanged by vigilantes, either in Virginia City or Bannack.

Is it possible that the energy from this violent past is still present in the town of approximately one hundred people? This and other theories have been advanced to explain why Virginia City still seems to have more than its share of untimely deaths, especially murders, and a plethora of paranormal phenomena. Some residents with whom I spoke mentioned a high rate of alcoholism and drug abuse as factors contributing to the high mortality rate, and former chief of police Mike Gordon said that, as the last surviving western boomtown of the 1860s, Virginia City has always attracted a number of ne'er-do-wells along with honest citizens.

"It's almost as if the whole place is possessed," said Lori Evans, a former costumer with the Virginia City Players, the oldest summer-stock company in Montana. Lori has heard the theory that gold dust gets under people's skin and makes them act differently, and actress Angela Rinaldi agrees that something about the town alters behavior.

"I spent four summers working at Virginia City, from 1984 to 1988, and I saw normally mild-mannered people fly into rages or behave in destructive ways there," she explained. "When you're in the town, you can feel an incredibly strong energy, and that energy has to go somewhere."

At no time was this energy more intense than in the aftermath of a

......

tragic accident in the summer of 1988. Actor Peter Walther clearly recalls the events of that Saturday night. "I had a slight case of the flu, so I went back to my cabin to lie down for half an hour between shows," he said. "Suddenly I heard a lot of commotion outside; it turned out that, just a short distance from my cabin, some guys in a jeep had missed a curve in the road coming down from the gulch. They rolled the vehicle and one of them was pinned underneath."

This man's head and neck were crushed, and he died a slow, agonizing death because rescue workers were not able to cut him free in time. In the hours following the wreck, at least four people reported strong vibrations of anger and fear, unexplained noises, and a general feeling of uneasiness near the site of the tragedy.

"You could just feel that poor kid furiously stomping around out there and refusing to accept the fact that he was dead," explained Patrick Judd, whose cabin was near where the accident had occurred. "Even my dog sensed that something was wrong, because he was unusually restless and kept growling all night."

Stacey Gordon's cabin was right next to the cabin of the man who died, and she remembers that neighborhood dogs barked frantically and ripped apart the garbage at the victim's house. "The dogs had always ignored the trash before, but that night they scattered things all over the place and made it look as if a hurricane had hit."

Virginia City has also been the scene of more traditional hauntings. At least eight buildings, many of them associated with the Virginia City Players, seem rife with psychic phenomena of all kinds.

The Opera House itself has been the setting for eerie events. When A. J. Kalanick and director Bill Koch first opened the building for the 1991 season, they were baffled to see that two of the lamps suspended from the ceiling were swinging, even though no one had been in the theater for a long time. Shortly after that, A. J. and Peter Walther heard phantom footsteps when they were getting the first show, *Frankenstein*, ready to go. Around three or four in the morning, the theater's back door opened, and both men plainly heard someone walk into the building.

"A. J. hollered hello, but there was no answer," Peter said. "We looked and saw that no one was there, and then the footsteps turned and walked back out and the door closed again. We just looked at each other and decided it was time to get out."

This was by no means the first time that A. J. had experienced unexplained phenomena in the theater. "I've often heard footsteps or laughter when I was the only one there, but the weirdest occurrence of this kind took place another morning around three o'clock," he said. "I was working on the set by myself when I heard a deep bass voice laughing in the middle of the house. All the lights were on and I looked around, but I saw no one. I thought someone was playing a joke, so I walked out to the lobby. Nobody was there, either. I walked back through the house and when I was right in the middle of it, I heard the same voice behind me, laughing again.

"I spun around, but no one was there," A. J. insisted. "By this time, I'd had enough and wanted to be left alone. I resumed working on the stage and picked up an electric drill to plug it into the socket. I was holding one end of the cord, and even though I was still five feet away from the outlet, I got a shock in my hand. I dropped the drill and fled the theater immediately. That was the first time I ever felt endangered by any kind of psychic occurrence."

Once, when A. J. and Bill Koch were working through a scene, Bill suddenly turned pale and announced that he'd seen a little spectral man standing in the corner and smiling at him. On another occasion Bill was greeted by the ghost of a dear friend who had died three summers before. "Larry was a seventy-six-year-old piano player from the Bale of Hay Saloon, and for a second I saw him standing on the stage at the Opera House," Bill said. "He wasn't trying to scare me—he just wanted to say hello."

Bill can't attribute the same friendly motive to a phantom that visited him in his basement apartment in the old rehearsal hall just up the hill from the Opera House. "This was 1985, when I was the stage manager," Bill explained. "I really got the heebie-jeebies staying in that room. Every night before I went to bed I pulled the stairwell door shut and locked it with a hook and eye, and then I locked my bedroom door with a bolt.

"One night I had just closed my eyes but hadn't fallen asleep yet when I heard the stairwell door open. There was no way anyone could have unlocked that door from the other side, but that's what happened. I heard someone walking down the stairs and over toward my bedroom. The bolted door came open easily without being forced and I heard footsteps entering my room and walking to the foot of my bed. I felt the presence of someone standing there but, when I looked, I could see no one. I felt this invisible someone sit down on the end of my bed and, just as the bed went down from the person's weight, I felt a heavy masculine hand reach over and touch my leg.

"I was absolutely terrified," Bill said. "I began saying the Lord's Prayer over and over in my mind while my heart was beating a million times a minute. Then I felt the hand leave my leg and the invisible person got up off of the bed. I heard him walk out of my room and shut the door, and then I heard his footsteps ascending the stairs. Needless to say, I didn't sleep the rest of the night but just sat in bed watching the door."

A former theater director once reported unexplained knocking on the door of another basement apartment in the same building. And Gerry Roe, who now teaches drama at Rocky Mountain College in Billings, stayed for a while in the old rehearsal hall in 1989 and never did get a good night's sleep.

"It was like a nightmare," he recalled. "It was almost as if something was trying to keep me awake. Of course, my anxiety might have had something to do with the fact that I was playing the demon barber who slits people's throats in *Sweeney Todd*."

Another haunted site well known to the Virginia City Players is the costume shop. When Lori Evans worked there, she heard that her predecessor had once felt as though she was sitting on someone's lap when she sat down in a chair to sew. Lori herself often heard phantom footsteps and a mysterious pounding, and once she heard a man clearing his throat when no one was there.

"About a week after that, I heard the same man humming, but I was alone in the shop," Lori said. "One time when Tim Gordon came looking for me, I had already gone and the lights were out. He called my name and heard a laugh, and he swore that it sounded like my voice, but of course the shop was empty."

Lori also had problems with costumes that disappeared and reappeared, usually when she was the only person in the shop. "I came across a child's dress that I'd never seen before, and when I went to show it to Angela Rinaldi, I couldn't find it," she explained. "The next time I went into the costume shop, the dress was in plain view. I tried a second time to show it to Angela, but it disappeared from the racks again."

Someone could have been playing tricks on Lori, but she doesn't think so. And it may be significant that the dress that seemed to move by itself was made for a child, because at least two people saw the ghosts of little girls in the vicinity of the costume shop.

"There's a beautiful yellow rosebush next to the shop, and one day I thought about picking some of the buds," A. J. Kalanick recalled. "But then I had the feeling that I shouldn't, and I got a sudden hunch that a little girl was buried there. Two or three weeks later, I was walking past the costume shop when I saw a blonde-haired child sitting on the porch. She looked six to eight years old and was wearing a full-length cornflower blue dress gathered around the neckline and a flat hat with a little bubble in the middle. I looked at her once and glanced away, and when I looked back there was no sign of her. I never did find out whether my hunch was correct about a child being buried near the rosebush."

Bill Koch also saw an apparition of a little girl standing beside the costume shop, but she was evidently not the one witnessed by A. J. "This one was crying her eyes out," Bill remembered, "and she seemed to be waiting for someone. She also appeared to be aware of my presence—in fact, I think I scared her. Her dark hair was braided and she was wearing a cream-colored peasant-type smock dress with flowered stitchery and long ruffled sleeves. She also wore a tiny apron. The odd thing was that she had no real color but was sepia-toned, like an old photograph. She looked very solid at first, but, as I watched her, she faded and disappeared."

Lori Evans saw a white specter on the porch of the costume shop and wonders if it might have been the ghostly nun who usually appears in some buildings known as the Bonanza House and the Bonanza Inn. "There was a nineteenth-century newspaper story about a white specter seen walking up the street at night," she said, "and I know I saw the same thing. I was staying in one of the cabins, and around three o'clock one morning I got up to go to the bathroom in the bathhouse.

"I happened to glance up the hill, and I saw a white figure sitting on the porch of the costume shop. At first I thought it was Stacey Gordon's cat, but as I kept looking I made out the small figure of a woman, or perhaps a little girl. What I saw was only an outline, a white aura, and I could clearly see that this person had one foot up on some rocks, her elbow on her knee, and her hand underneath her chin. She was very relaxed, and I could tell that she was watching me.

"I hurried in and out of the bathhouse without looking again toward the costume shop. But all the way back to my cabin I could feel the apparition watching me.

"About a week later, a piano player for one of the other companies told me that she too had seen the same white figure watching her," said Lori. "It may or may not be significant that both of us had this experience on a Monday night."

Even though Lori thought the figure might have been the ghostly nun, its small size and the fact that it was on the porch of the costume shop indicates that it may have been one of the phantom children. But since its features were indistinct, there is no way to know.

The spectral nun that Lori thought she saw, along with the other phantoms of the Bonanza House and Bonanza Inn, are some of the best-known spooks in town. According to John Ellingsen, curator of the restoration project in Virginia City, the Bonanza Inn was built to be the county courthouse. When a new courthouse was built in 1876, some nuns bought the first one and turned it into a Catholic hospital. They then built what is now the Bonanza House for a nunnery. Both structures have been used to house actors for the summer season, and they have probably been the settings for more paranormal phenomena than any other buildings in Virginia City.

One room in the Bonanza Inn was even nailed shut because of all the frightening things that occurred there. Lin Magee was a maid at the inn in the mid-1970s, and she often had problems in that room. "My boss always called the ghost Melissa because she thought it was a nice name," Lin recalled. "But what the ghost did wasn't so nice—I would hang the towels neatly and turn around again to find them all rumpled up. As soon as I put soap in the room it would disappear. And I'd make the bed just to have someone mess it up again. And all these things happened when I was the only person in the room."

During this same period, the film *The Missouri Breaks,* starring Marlon Brando and Jack Nicholson, was being shot in nearby Nevada City, and one of the crew stayed in the Bonanza Inn. "All night long he heard somebody knocking on his door and window," John Ellingsen told me, "but every time he went to check, no one was there. Finally he went out to sleep in his car. He complained the next day that his neighbors were too noisy, and that's when he learned that he'd been the only one in the building. This guy was supposed to stay there a month, but he moved out promptly and got a room in Ennis."

It's unlikely that the ghostly nun was to blame for any of these disturbances, because even after death she has continued her role as a healer and a comforter of the sick. The many tales about her are all similar and, because they come from people who in many cases don't know one another, they are more convincing than the average ghost story.

When Angela Rinaldi lived in the Bonanza House, both she and a housemate encountered the phantom nun under different circumstances. "It was my first summer in Virginia City, and we were preparing to open our show," Angela remembered. "Because of the dryness and high elevation, as well as the fact that I was singing about ten hours a day, I was very hoarse and afraid that I wouldn't have a voice for opening night. The stress of worrying just made matters worse, and I tried everything I could think of to make my throat better.

"Just a couple of nights before the show was to open, I could barely talk, let alone sing. I went to bed and prayed I wouldn't let everyone down by not having a voice. As usual, my roommate and I kept the bedroom door closed because it helped to keep our room warmer.

"I fell asleep but was awakened shortly afterward by the growling of my toy poodle, Rufus," Angela continued. "I saw that the bedroom door was wide open, and that struck me as odd because it's a very heavy door and we always had to shove to get it open. As I stared at the doorway, I saw an outline of a person. It was a shadow in the shape of someone wearing a long robe or hood, with no legs showing.

"At first I wasn't sure what I was seeing, and I must have kept my eyes on the form for about thirty seconds. When I finally realized I was looking at an apparition, I got scared and closed my eyes. When I looked again, the figure was gone.

"The next day, I realized that a small miracle had occurred," Angela explained. "My voice was back and I never had problems with it again. After talking to several people about what I saw, I'm convinced that it was the ghostly nun who came back to cure my throat."

Angela's housemate, an actor named Chris, was also visited by the phantom sister after he fell on one of Virginia City's rain-slick wooden boardwalks. "He couldn't catch himself with his hands because he had them in his pockets," Angela recalled, "so he landed right on his face and broke his nose. His glasses also broke and cut his face, and he ended up needing five stitches over his eye. Even worse, he suffered a minor concussion.

"Chris insisted he felt well enough to go on stage, so we modified that night's performance so he didn't have to do a lot of moving around. As soon as the show was over he came home and went straight to bed. The rest of us were still downstairs at midnight, and we heard Chris talking up in his room. We couldn't make out what he said, but the doctor had told us he might be slightly delirious, so we weren't worried.

"The next morning Chris woke up refreshed, with his dizziness gone. He told us he'd spent an incredible night talking with Sister Theresa, who told him he was going to be fine and that she would be there to help if he needed anything.

The boardwalk on Wallace Street in Virginia City, the "Ghost Capital" of Montana.
(© M. J. Gordon)

"We all just looked at each other and didn't know what to say," Angela admitted. "Chris was a real cutup, and we didn't always take him seriously, but he finally convinced us that he was telling the truth. He said, 'I know what I saw, and whether I was delirious or not, I know I talked to her.' And we had to admit that he had a very speedy recovery and he didn't even get a scar."

The visitations of the ghostly nun helped to reassure Angela that at least some of the spooks in the Bonanza House were benign. And she desperately needed such reassurances, because strange things had begun happening the moment she drove in from Seattle.

As she brought in things from her car, the front door she'd left open kept closing itself, and the volume of her radio kept fluctuating. Later that evening, coming back from the Opera House, she was unable to open the front door even though it no longer had a lock and normally swung open with a simple turn of the handle.

"Even when I tugged and pushed, the door wouldn't open," Angela recalled. "And a light I'd left on in the living room was off. I finally decided I wasn't meant to spend that night in the house, so I went to sleep at a friend's cabin.

"After this first day, it became more and more obvious that the Bonanza House was haunted," Angela explained. "Keys disappeared from where my housemates and I had left them, and we spent a lot of time looking for things that had been moved. One night about a week after my arrival, I woke up to the sound of my roommate Maureen calling me. She had seen a man sitting on my bed, and when she sat up to observe him more closely, he evaporated into the ceiling.

"In spite of her terror, Maureen was able to describe the apparition very specifically. He was wearing wire-rimmed glasses and a shirt, ascot, trousers, and boots from the nineteenth century. He was looking blankly at her, and when she called my name, his image became wavy, as if she were seeing it under water. Then it seemed to float up and disappear."

It was Angela's turn to see the apparition next. One night she sat upright in bed, certain that something was wrong. "I looked over at Maureen, who was sleeping on her side facing me. I was just starting to lie back down again when I noticed the figure of a man lying in bed with her, next to the wall. He was on his stomach and he pushed himself up onto his hands, looked over at me, and smiled lecherously.

"I was beside myself," Angela confessed, "shaking so badly that I couldn't even call Maureen's name. When I was finally able to wake her, we compared notes and were positive we'd seen the same man. He looked real but transparent, and when I saw him, his expression was cocky and defiant. I know he meant to scare me and he did a good job."

Fortunately, neither woman saw the leering ghost again, but other types of eerie phenomena began occurring almost daily. When Angela and Maureen came home to rest at lunchtime, they often found their clothing and shoes strewn all over the bedroom; it looked as if someone had tried them on.

"Chris lived in the upstairs bedroom, and he never had his clothes tampered with, but he often heard a woman's voice calling his name from the banister," Angela explained. "Several times he came to ask what we wanted, but neither Maureen nor I had called him. This was especially irksome because it usually happened early in the morning, before any of us had gotten up."

For Angela, however, the most alarming occurrences were those involving her dog, Rufus. Many times when the small poodle walked across the living room, he yelped in pain and acted as if he had been hit or stepped on. "He hated being alone in the house," Angela said. "Sometimes when I came home, I found him barking so frantically he could barely catch his breath, so I started taking him with me everywhere.

"Once he had a bloody scab, about the size of the tip of my little finger, on top of his head. I thought maybe he had a tick embedded in his skin, but the veterinarian believed the scab to be the result of his being hit over the head with a blunt object.

"The poor thing was constantly tormented," Angela continued. "Once some people came over after a show and one skeptic in the crowd said, 'If it takes all night, I'm going to stay here until I see something spooky.' As soon as the words were out of his mouth, the dog went flying across the room, just as if someone had kicked him. The skeptic said, 'Okay, I'm going now,' and he never came back."

Once, when Angela and Rufus were alone in the house, their afternoon nap was disturbed when the dog's rubber ball began bouncing all over the living room—apparently by itself!

Another time, after a show, Angela came home with the dog and almost fell over an invisible barrier on the porch steps. "The energy was so strong that I felt as if I'd bounced off of something," she said. "But I went on into the house and began washing off my stage makeup. The water was on full blast, but I still heard someone walking down the stairs from Chris's bedroom.

"It was dark up there, and I knew that no one else was home, but I called out anyway. I got no response, so I turned the water back on. Again I heard footsteps coming down the stairs, and it sounded as if they were made by a person wearing heavy work boots. I yelled again, 'Chris, if that's you, you're not funny.' I heard two more steps and then I grabbed the dog and ran out the front door. When I got to the bar, Chris was there, and he swore he hadn't been anywhere near the house."

One day Angela was reading in the living room when she felt someone push her out of her chair. On another occasion, she saw the shadow of a hangman's noose projected onto the wall, which itself seemed to lighten from a peach shade to white. Angela insists that there were no trees or anything else near the window that could have cast a shadow, and no trick of light could have made the wall appear to change color.

When Angela's parents came to visit, they also were treated to the supernatural phenomena of the Bonanza House. Her mother reported that her bed was shaking, and neither trains nor earthquakes were to blame. And when Angela's boyfriend stayed in the house, he and Angela both had an experience that defies explanation. Each one at a different time during the night looked down toward the floor and saw what appeared to be many mattresses stacked on top of one another. No floor was visible beneath them.

"Even if we were both dreaming, why did we have the same dream?" Angela asked, adding that before she saw the mattresses, she noticed that the room seemed to have changed in appearance. "The neighbor had a floodlight in her backyard, so even at night I could see colors. That night, the walls were an ash blue, and pictures in oval wooden frames seemed to have replaced the posters I had put up. I looked around the room for a few seconds wondering if I were dreaming, but I know I was awake."

Angela's twin sister Katie also came to visit, and she's convinced that one of the entities in the Bonanza House followed her back to Seattle. "Three or four times I had what seemed like a very real dream, in which a woman wearing a flowered, old-fashioned western dress with a bustle stood in my room and smiled in a demonic way at me," Katie said. "She had brown ringlets and dark eyes and she seemed so real, especially the time she tried to strangle me. That's when I yelled for her to leave me alone, and I never saw her again."

Chris's friend Jerry lived in the upstairs room during Angela's fourth season in the Bonanza House, and he often felt an unseen someone tugging at his shirt or tapping him on the shoulder. As had Chris, he also heard a woman's voice calling his name from the stairwell.

"One night when he'd gone to bed early, he kept coming downstairs to tell us to quit bothering him," Angela recalled. "He said that someone kept calling his name, but we pleaded our innocence. About an hour after his first complaint, he came running downstairs in his underwear, so scared that he hadn't even taken time to put on his bathrobe. He said that from the wall right behind the headboard of his bed he'd heard persistent knocking, as if someone were trying to get his attention. None of us could have been making the sound from downstairs, and no trees are close enough to brush against the house."

Some time later, during a dinner party, Angela took snapshots and when the prints were developed she was surprised to find one showing a reflection of a man's face in a mirror. If anyone had been reflected in the mirror, it would have been Angela herself, because she was standing right in front of it when she took the picture.

"The mystery man looked like the ghostly fellow that Maureen and I saw that first week in our bedroom," Angela claimed, "although some people thought the reflection was of Joel, the bartender. I don't agree that it looks like Joel, and I don't see how he could have appeared in the mirror anyway, because he was nowhere near me when I took the picture.

"One night we did try to find out why the Bonanza House was haunted," Angela continued. "We used a Ouija board and we contacted a six-year-old girl who identified herself as E-L-I- before the letters became gibberish. I thought maybe she just couldn't spell and that her name might have been Elizabeth. We weren't any more enlightened about the cause of the phenomena, but after we used the Ouija board our clothes stopped being scattered around."

Angela recalled one other incident she'd heard about that took place at either the Bonanza House or the Bonanza Inn. "The story was that a woman used profanity and was slapped soundly but invisibly across the face," she said. "Everyone supposedly saw a red hand-mark appear on her skin. It's interesting to speculate that the ghostly nun was just registering her disapproval."

Phantom ladies have also been reported at another summer home for actors, the Ironrod Cabin. Taken from a settlement by the same name, the cabin has long had the reputation of being haunted, although little is known of its history.

Actor Brian King was almost asleep there one night in 1977 when the door opened and closed and someone walked toward his bed. Startled, Brian jumped up and the figure vanished. When he checked the door, he found it still locked.

Brian never knew the sex of the spectral being who entered his cabin, but when Lori Evans stayed there in 1985 she saw clearly that her nocturnal guest was female. "I woke up to see what appeared to be a servant lady standing at the foot of my bed," Lori recalled. "She wore a dress with a white apron and her hair was pulled back in a bun. What I remember most vividly, though, is the weird smile on her face. I was so scared that I pulled the covers up over my head."

A. J. Kalanick stayed in the Ironrod Cabin in 1989, and his experiences were even more bizarre. One afternoon he returned to the locked cabin to find his bookcase tipped over and books scattered across the room. The next day, while he was outside talking to a friend no more than forty feet from the cabin, a wooden tape rack fell off the wall and tapes were scattered all over the floor.

"I should have heard the rack and tapes falling, but I didn't," A. J. said. "Another time, I came back to find the television on, even though I'd turned it off before I left."

But these events were just a prelude to the far more dramatic occurrences later that summer. "I was lying down for a few minutes before going to the Opera House," he explained, "when the cabin door opened and a woman in a long red Victorian dress strolled in with a German shepherd dog on a leash. She just stood there smiling at me, and when I sat up she faded away. I got up to check the door and found it locked.

"Two or three nights later, I came straight back to the cabin after the show," A. J. continued. "I had just turned the lights off and was lying in bed when the same woman in the red dress walked up to my bed from the other room.

"The odd thing was that she appeared to be illuminated. She didn't radiate light to anything else, but every detail of the woman herself was clear. She still had the dog on its leather leash, and this time I noticed that in her other hand she was holding a quill pen. She smiled at me in the same strange way as before, and when I asked her who she was, she turned and walked back into the other room before disappearing.

"About a week later, I woke up in the middle of the night and sensed that someone was in the room. I opened my eyes and saw the woman standing at the foot of the bed, smiling at me in that same odd way.

If I were an artist, I could draw a perfectly detailed picture, because this time the image remained for about fifteen seconds. The red dress was trimmed in lace and was tight under the bust, and the skirt was full under the V-shaped bodice. The woman was very pretty, with a fair complexion and high cheekbones, and she wore her light brown hair pulled back into a netted snood. She had dropped the German shepherd's leash, but the dog was still standing next to her. In her right hand she held the quill pen, white with black shading toward the tip.

"But this time I saw something I'd never noticed before," A. J. continued. "Superimposed on top of the pen was a transparent dagger. It had a two-sided blade and a black handle with a gold top. Puzzled and alarmed, I asked the lady what she wanted, but she didn't answer—she just stood there and smiled at me. I reached over to turn on the light beside my bed and she vanished.

"I was really worried that I was going crazy, but I believed that the ghostly woman was trying to tell me something," A. J. explained. "I decided I would ask her to come back. For a week, I asked her to return, but she never did."

The ghostly lady was gone, but the psychic phenomena didn't end. One night Peter Walther was going to the community bathhouse when he saw a strange being looking in the window of A. J.'s cabin.

"It was a tall black shadowy figure on this otherwise bright night," Peter remembered. "It turned and looked at me and then looked back into the window. I just kept walking and went on into the bathhouse. On the way back to my cabin, I refused to look in the direction of A. J.'s place again until I'd gotten quite a distance away. When I did look back, the shadowy figure was still standing there."

The Lightning Splitter is another Virginia City house with a decidedly sinister reputation. Originally a brothel, the unusual structure was named for its three highly pitched gables. The gable farthest back is one of the highest points in town and is frequently struck by lightning.

Tim Gordon's brother Mike lived in the house for several years, and he admits that he never felt comfortable there, especially while working in the kitchen, which he had turned into a darkroom. "I was always particularly uneasy when I was working at the sink," Mike confessed, "feeling that I was being watched from the stairway. But the most frightening thing occurred one night when I was sleeping downstairs.

"I dreamed that I woke up to find that the wallpaper and furniture had been changed. I dreamed this three times, and three times I also dreamed that I awoke with a terrible pain in my back. It felt as if something were biting me, and in the dream I was reaching around to fight off my attacker. The third time I really did wake up, and the pain in my back was all too real and my hand was actually striking something solid. I felt that whatever I was hitting was made of flesh and blood, some large animal perhaps, and it didn't want to stop biting.

"I was groggy at first, but when I realized what was happening, I baled out of bed and looked for whatever had been attacking me," Mike explained. "There was no animal in the room, but I know I wasn't imagining things because there were red marks all over my back. I was completely unnerved by this experience even though I've never believed in the supernatural."

Mike wonders if his strange experience had something to do with a former inhabitant of the house with whom he had had a disagreement. This man, who was later killed in a motorcycle accident, had apparently dabbled in witchcraft and satanism, and he was one of Virginia City's most unsavory characters, proud of his reputation as a bar fighter and drug dealer. Before Mike moved into the Lightning Splitter, he argued with this disreputable fellow, who threatened that he had "left something in the house" for him. Some evidence suggests that the "something" might have left the house occasionally, because Bill Koch and Peter Walther, in two separate incidents, reported being chased one summer night by an invisible doglike creature. Both men were en route to the Lightning Splitter at the time.

When Mike's sister Vicky came to visit with her three-year-old son, the little boy kept saying that the Lightning Splitter had an evil beast upstairs. Vicky believes that her son's claim may have been more than childish imagination at work because she, too, sensed a presence in the house. "One night when we were sleeping downstairs," Vicky recalled, "I woke up and asked my son if he was awake. In my mind, I sensed the voice of a man nearby saying, 'No, but I am!'"

Tim and Stacey Gordon lived in the house after Mike, and they reported having frequent nightmares there. Stacey's dreams often involved a child, and Mike heard a rumor from someone in town that a child had, indeed, died violently at the house.

On one occasion Stacey saw what she described as a "long, white, orb-like thing" float past her in the kitchen. "I don't know what this apparition was," she said, "but it came down the stairwell, which was always cold and creepy. And when we had guests staying upstairs they often reported hearing footsteps on the landing."

One evening, while Stacey was at the theater, Tim was at home in the Lightning Splitter with his friends Pam Koch and Lori Evans. They decided to go into town for a beer, and before leaving the house Tim pulled the plug on a lamp that was flickering. It was several hours later that he mentioned unplugging the lamp to Stacey.

"She gave me a funny look and told me that there couldn't have been any light on," Tim explained, "because the bulb had been gone from the lamp for quite a while."

A little nervous about remaining in the house that night, Tim and Stacey went to visit Bill and Pam Koch. When Bill heard the latest ghost story from the Lightning Splitter, he said, "Thank God nothing weird has ever happened in this house"—and as if on cue a picture fell off of the wall.

Earlier residents of the Lightning Splitter reported seeing a phantom woman in a chair, and Tim Gordon learned that an occupant after himself had stripped the wallpaper, gone to lunch, and returned to find the wallpaper back on the walls.

For reasons still not understood, Virginia City appears to be a magnet for psychic energy, leading many who have spent time there to claim that the whole town is haunted. Even natural formations are affected, as is evident from a bizarre experience shared by Lori Evans and A. J. Kalanick.

In the summer of 1988, they experienced the same thing at the same time but in different buildings. Around three o'clock one morning, both of them awakened to an eerie moaning from outside that didn't sound as if it were coming from a person or an animal.

"I grew up on a farm," A. J. explained, "and I've heard all kinds of natural sounds, from wild animals as well as domestic ones. But this sound had an unearthly tone to it, and it seemed to surround everything. The oddest thought popped into my head—that the hills themselves were crying. At breakfast the next day, I found out that Lori Evans had heard the same weird sound and had had the same strange thought."

Is Virginia City so full of psychic energy that even the hills reverberate with it? Something very unusual is occurring there, and parapsychologists owe it to themselves to investigate this wonderland of the supernatural.

Three
....

The Wicked Wench of Clore Street

R esidents of early-day Montana could sometimes be an unsavory lot, and often their only motives in coming West were to fleece the more honest settlers who were also trying to establish lives on the frontier. These opportunists were especially attracted to mining towns, where enormous amounts of wealth could be made, lost, and stolen in a relatively short period of time. And while these villains were certainly not folks most of us would want for neighbors, no one can deny that they left behind some of the most compelling stories of the Old West.

On page one of the *Great Falls Tribune* of June 11, 1885, there is a short article titled "A Haunted House," apparently written by a correspondent from the *Helena Independent* and referring to "some very mysterious occurrences" that had recently taken place in Helena "in a deserted cabin on Clore Street." (It seems logical to assume that the same article ran in the *Independent* at about the same time, although I was unable to find a copy of it.) The unnamed correspondent writes that the strange and unaccountable phenomena were known to be in some way associated with the old cabin itself and included "shrieks of apparently suffering persons, groans, rappings on the door, white specters instantly disappearing in the air, etc."

Even the police became involved in the mystery when shortly after midnight a patrolman making his accustomed rounds near the cabin heard the horrible groans of someone inside who was obviously in the throes of death. Fearing that a murder was being committed, the policeman lost no time in breaking into the cabin. Inside it was pitch black, so he lit a match. To his utter amazement, however, the cabin was completely empty!

The newspaper correspondent then writes that an oldtimer had been able to supply a clue regarding the cabin's grisly history. During the heyday of the mining camps, the small shanty had been occupied by an old woman suspected of murdering "more than one unfortunate" who had struck it rich. More identification of the woman is not given, but the oldtimer did remember that the evidence of foul play was so damning against her that she was "notified by 3-7-77 to 'pack her kit and ship,'" which she apparently did.

More than one hundred years later we are left wondering whether the woman was a prostitute or just an exceptionally greedy and unscrupulous landlady. And although she was able to leave the cabin, the tortured echoes of her victims seem to have remained behind.

The correspondent ends the article in a way that confuses more than it enlightens: "Since the first experience of the officer others have been keeping close watch of the haunted cabin, and it is asserted a reasonable explanation found for these mysterious happenings. We hope to give a satisfactory solution of the problem in our next—*Helena Independent.*"

Does this mean that a "reasonable" explanation for the phenomena was found by the officers and that the correspondent is waiting for the next issue of the newspaper to print it? Or does it mean that the officers were merely hoping to discover a logical explanation for the screams and ghostly white specters witnessed in the Clore Street cabin?

Sadly for us, the answer must remain a tantalizing mystery, because apparently no other clippings relating to the matter have survived in the files of the Montana Historical Society, or in any other archives that were searched for ghost stories. Perhaps a future researcher will stumble upon another such article, if it does exist.

Or perhaps the hauntings are still going on in the same spot where the murderous wench finished off her victims and their screams are yet to be heard in the dark of night.

Four

Ghostly Garnet

It's ironic that Garnet, the best-preserved ghost town in Montana, was never built to last. Gold miners intent on making quick fortunes weren't interested in constructing houses, stores, and saloons sturdy enough to weather the decades. Instead, they wasted little time in erecting temporary shelters, often with no foundation but the bare ground, before returning to the far more important task of extracting minerals from the surrounding mountains. For who could predict how long it would be before the rich deposits played out and it was time to move on again?

Yet, almost one hundred years after the founding of the town in 1895, quite a few of those hastily built structures remain, lovingly restored and protected by the Garnet Preservation Association and the Bureau of Land Management (BLM). Kelly's Saloon, the J. K. Wells Hotel, the blacksmith shop, several of the miners' cabins, and other buildings still stand in Garnet. Only the people who lived and worked in them have gone—but not without leaving some psychic echoes behind.

After the BLM took on the job of protecting the town from further decay and vandalism, it hired Michael Gordon to serve as caretaker during the winter of 1971–1972. For a four- or five-day period that season the temperature plummeted and held steady at thirty degrees below zero, so cold that snow took on the consistency of sugar and never packed down so that snowmobiles could travel on it.

It was on one of these bitterly cold nights that Mike heard the strains of honky-tonk music coming from one of the buildings. Believing himself to be the only person in town, he was puzzled, but he decided that some cross-country skiers or snowshoers must have come into Garnet without his knowledge. He set off in the direction of some cabins to look for them but turned back when he realized that the music was coming from somewhere else.

"I finally traced it to Kelly's Saloon, a typical false-fronted building constructed before the turn of the century," Mike explained. "It's true that extremely cold weather can alter sounds, but as I approached the saloon I had no doubt that I was hearing the noise of a rip-roaring party.

"I walked a plank from the hillside up to the back door, and the sounds got louder. I opened the door and walked onto a landing where a stairway used to be. No doubt about it—people were talking and laughing and a piano was being played. I walked over to where a railing used to be and looked down into the bar area.

"The sounds stopped as if someone had switched off a radio," he said, "and the old saloon was empty except for a few odd pieces of furniture scattered about. I realized that what I had heard did not belong to the present time, but for some reason I wasn't frightened."

Mike and a later caretaker, Kerry Moon, had never heard of one another before I began my research, but their experiences involving the saloon were uncannily alike. Kerry was the caretaker at Garnet during the mid-1970s; during his stay he enjoyed the company of Whiskers, a border collie-sheltie mix once owned by a previous caretaker who had died. One night in the middle of December 1975, Whiskers began barking and howling.

"He woke me up, and that's when I heard the sounds of music and laughter coming from Kelly's Saloon," Kerry remembered. "I was worried because I thought teenagers or transients had found their way there and were having a party. Determined to evict them, I grabbed my rifle and Whiskers and I walked the eighty feet from the guard cabin to the old saloon.

"The ragtime music and voices were loud and clear, and as we got closer I could even hear glasses clinking together. But just as soon as Whiskers touched his nose to the building, all the sounds stopped.

"I couldn't believe my ears, and when I went inside to check, the old saloon was empty," Kerry confessed. "What bothered me the most was that I had definitely heard a piano playing, and there was no such thing there. In fact, Kelly's hadn't had one for years."

Kerry heard the same ghostly noises coming from the saloon on several other occasions and, whenever he attempted to investigate them, they disappeared. "They usually occurred between midnight and three A.M.," he said, "but I also heard them at other times when the town was quiet. Even in the summer, the fire crew woke me up now and then to complain about the loud parties going on at Kelly's. My brother Colin and other guests heard the sounds, too. I knew there was no point in checking the saloon again, but I did so just to satisfy people. Naturally, I never found anyone inside."

Once Kerry tried to fool what he referred to as "the good-time spirits of Garnet." On a fine September afternoon he and his six-year-old son Nathan left town, then sneaked back four hours later hoping to catch the ghosts unaware.

"We were pretty sure that no living people would be in town that evening, so we thought the spooks would appreciate the quiet," he explained. "For nearly an hour we waited silently in the shadow of a big ponderosa pine, and then the clamor began. We heard just a little at first, a few laughs and some glasses clinking together. And then came the sounds of rough ragtime piano music.

"Nate asked who was making all the ruckus, so I said, 'Let's go find out.' We walked down the hill, and just as we got to the building, the noises stopped. Nate was confused and began to cry, and I felt pretty uncomfortable myself, because once again I realized that I wasn't dealing with a material threat."

An amateur scientist, Kerry has a theory that may help explain the sounds emanating from the deserted saloon. "I believe that the many crystalline formations in the Garnet Range might somehow receive radio waves and that the dense mineral deposits in the area might act as speakers," he explained. "The miners drove many long metal shafts, rods, and pipes into the quartz formations for ventilation and water removal, and these may also act as antennae. Perhaps the sounds from the saloon are resonating from this mixture of quartz, other minerals, and the metal shafts. If the town of Garnet really is a big radio receiver, the music and voices are audible because they are real and could probably be recorded."

Kerry once tried to do just that with a microphone attached to a small tape recorder, but it picked up only background noise. He believes that better equipment probably would have recorded the sounds more clearly. "Of course, I suppose it's also possible that the music and voices really are coming to us from the past," he said. "Or perhaps the spirits of Garnet are in there celebrating their lost way of life, when the town was a booming mecca for the miners of the last Montana gold rush."

As plausible as this theory may be, Kerry has none to explain the mysterious caller whom he heard walking up to his cabin and knocking on the door just before midnight. When Kerry opened the door no one was there, and the only footprints in the snow were those leading up *to* the porch—but none leading away.

Unexplained footsteps are nothing new to the current caretaker of

Garnet, Dwight Gappert, who has heard the sounds of walking and doors shutting inside buildings known to be empty. "For one thing, most of these old structures no longer have doors," he explained. "And one of the more frequently heard noises is that of people walking up the staircase to the second story inside the Wells Hotel. The stairway has about thirty steps, so there's a definite recognizable pattern to the footsteps. And whenever you approach the buildings, the noises stop."

Dwight said that most of the unexplained sounds he has heard occur either at daybreak or at dusk. He remembers one woman who had a very frightening experience after leaving her rental cabin just after the sun had gone down. "It was quite a jaunt from her cabin to the restroom," he recalled. "And on her way back to the cabin she noticed two people walking up the street. She called to them but they didn't answer. And then she noticed that their clothing was old-fashioned and that the gentleman was wearing bib overalls.

"She continued following them up the main street, which had only a few buildings still standing. They approached the hotel and went inside; the woman following them heard the sounds of a piano playing and people dancing.

"She ran the rest of the way back to her cabin and told her husband what had happened," Dwight said. "They grabbed a flashlight and returned to the hotel, only to find the front door locked and no sign of music or dancing."

John Ellingsen, a former curator and one of the directors of the preservation project, had his own spooky experience at the old hotel. He was taking measurements there in the summer of 1970 accompanied by a German shepherd dog belonging to John Crouch, the other director. Suddenly the dog ran frantically from the building, barking hysterically.

"At first I thought he'd probably heard a pack rat," John said, "but as I stood there and listened, I heard what sounded like human footsteps up on the top floor. The dog refused to go into the hotel after that.

"A year later, I had another scare at the same place," he continued. "I was in Garnet with a group of high school kids, and we'd spent much of the evening telling ghost stories and getting all psyched up. There were about eight of us, and we decided to take a flashlight to the hotel to see if we could find any spirits.

"It was a spooky night with the moon shining, and we walked out through the woods. The hotel was all boarded up back then, so we had to enter it through the back door. We started up the stairs with the flashlight and passed the second floor. But just as we got to the third floor, the flashlight went out.

"You should have heard all the screaming," John said, laughing. "We thought the ghost had gotten us, but a bigger danger was that somebody would fall through one of the holes in the floor. By groping along in the dark, we all got out of there in one piece.

"I had decided that the flashlight going off while we were inside the hotel was just a coincidence," John said, "until it came on again the second we walked out the door."

Al Wahlin is another person who has spent a great deal of time in Garnet, both as a summer visitor and as a former caretaker. He admitted that he has often wandered around the town late at night hoping to stir up the ghosts but having no luck. One night he thought he heard mysterious voices talking in another building, but then he realized that the sound was merely the buzzing of flies trapped between the trim and the window.

Al did experience a bona fide eerie encounter one spring day in 1978 or 1979 when the ice and snow were breaking up and melting off. "That time of year was especially nice," he said, "because usually no one came to town and I had the whole place to myself. I had been working on some project up in the shop, and I was about halfway back to my cabin when something made me glance over my shoulder.

"I saw a man, a woman, and a small child walking about thirty yards behind me. I hadn't talked to anybody for a week or two, and I was surprised to see them. I decided it would be nice to find out what they were doing in Garnet, so I turned around again to call to them—and no one was there.

"I couldn't figure out where they could have gotten to so quickly, especially as they were strolling along with the child between them, and the middle of the street was the only place where the snow was packed well enough to walk. I checked behind bushes and everywhere else I could think of, even going off on little side trails before convincing myself that I was the only person in town. And when I looked for footprints, the only ones I saw were the distinctive waffle patterns made by my own boots.

"Nothing seemed to be unusual about these people," Al insisted. "They were dressed normally for winter and they looked like a modern family, not inhabitants of early-day Garnet. The woman, for example, was wearing pants instead of a dress. I don't know who they were or how they managed to get out of sight so fast."

The front of Garnet's J. K. Wells Hotel, where phantoms have been heard climbing the stairs, playing an old piano, and dancing. *(Courtesy Bureau of Land Management, U.S. Department of the Interior)*

Al's desire to experience the unexplained at Garnet was rewarded on one other occasion, and he later learned that his wife, Gloria, had had an identical experience at the same place on a different evening. "It was winter sometime in the early 1980s," Al explained, "and we had rented a cabin known as the Dahl House. I woke up one night to see a glowing light floating over the woodstove in the center of the room. The whitish yellow light was about the size of a soccer ball, and after a while it rose to a distance of about five feet and began moving toward me. Then it floated up to a corner of the room above my head and disappeared.

"I wasn't really frightened, but I was puzzled, and I know I wasn't dreaming. I didn't find out that Gloria had seen exactly the same thing in the same place until we both began talking about the odd things that happen in Garnet."

Those "odd things" certainly are well documented, for in addition to appearing in this book, Garnet has been featured in D. F. Curran's *True Hauntings in Montana* and in Earl Murray's *Ghosts of the Old West*. Perhaps the ultimate irony of this town not built to last is just how permanent its ghostly inhabitants appear to be.

Five

The House of Screams

Unquestionably the spookiest house in Missoula, and probably in the entire state of Montana, is the turn-of-the-century residence at 319 South Fifth Street West. The house has a well-documented history of psychic phenomena over the past fifty years, and it claims the distinction of being one of very few structures in the state to have been exorcised, possibly more than once.

The house gained national publicity in an article in *Fate* in August 1975 (28: 76–80). Written by Henriette Lambros about the experience of her sister's family, "Our Ghost was a Scream" chronicles the weird events that troubled James and Eleanor Zakos when they bought the house and moved in during the late 1930s.

Almost immediately, James and Eleanor, their six children, and Eleanor's mother began hearing bloodcurdling screams that seemed to come from inside the rooms themselves. The horrible shrieking occurred at all hours of the day and night, starting at a low pitch and then getting higher and higher until the volume threatened to split the walls. The screams always came in pairs, and the voice was that of a woman in torment.

The dreadful screeching made life miserable for the family, and sleep was often impossible. Once, in the middle of the night, James got so angry that he grabbed a gun and searched the house, but he found nothing that could explain the unearthly noise.

Over the next few months, the troubled family did everything in their power to locate the source of the screams. They asked the police, the fire department, and an electrician to inspect the house from top to bottom, even checking for animals under the foundation and for branches scraping against the roof, but no one discovered anything out of the ordinary. Wondering if prowlers were somehow to blame, the Zakos family installed a yard light to scare them away, and Eleanor asked Henriette to take the dog for a few weeks to find out whether it could be making the noise. But no matter what the family did, the appalling screams continued.

Henriette knew that her sister's family was being pushed to the breaking point, but until she heard the mysterious shrieks herself she had a hard time believing they were real. One afternoon in September 1941, she was alone in the house with Eleanor and the new baby, Mary, who was herself to play a tragic role in the history of the house. Then came the sound that Henriette would never forget:

> As I recall we weren't talking at the moment that, into the quiet of that room, came the most horrible piercing scream I have ever heard. It was so loud the walls seemed to shake. It stopped a second, then came again louder than before. Then all was quiet.
>
> I honestly believe no human being could scream that loud. I believe it was superhuman, if such a thing is possible. It seemed to come from right outside the bedroom door.

Henriette goes on to say that the memory of the scream haunted her for months, but since her sister's family didn't want to move, they eventually resigned themselves to the ghastly sounds and did their best to ignore them.

At this time no one in the family had ever heard of exorcism, but an unusual sequence of events ultimately led to one being performed. In 1946, Henriette's husband, John, became terminally ill and Eleanor introduced him to a minister, Andrew Landin, who had a reputation for healing. Although the preacher was unsuccessful in curing the sick man, he became a good friend of the family, and after John's death the two sisters began attending Landin's church, The Light of the World Tabernacle. The friendship grew over the years, and, in the fall of 1956 the sisters finally told Landin about the terrible screams in the Zakos house. The minister's immediate response was that they were caused by the devil and the remedy would be to perform an exorcism.

Landin requested that the entire family be present for the occasion. He told everyone to join hands, and they all walked through every room of the house as the minister chanted and prayed for deliverance from the screams. Landin performed the ritual only once, and when it was over he assured the family that no one would ever hear the terrible sounds again.

The *Fate* article was written eighteen years after the exorcism, and Henriette Lambros reported that the home had been left in peace all that time. But even though the mysterious screams did not return, eerie phenomena of other kinds occurred after the magazine article was published.

In 1980, Steve Smith wrote a piece about the house for the *Missoulian*, focusing on thirty-eight-year-old Mary Zakos, who had been a baby when her aunt Henriette heard the screams. Mary was a self-professed writer of "light pornography" for confession magazines and, as was probably to be expected from someone who had been born in and spent most of her life in a haunted house, her specialty was horror fiction. She turned out stories with titles such as "Virgin Sacrifice: Satan Was My Sex Teacher," and she admitted to a fascination with cemeteries and gory movies.

The *Missoulian* article, titled "Mary Zakos, Mary Zakos," noted that she often felt a presence in her bedroom at night, and that on several occasions she had literally seen handwriting appear on the walls. "It looks like names and phone numbers," Mary was quoted as saying. "I won't put my glasses on or my contacts in when I see that writing. It scares me. It's weird. I'm afraid it's some kind of warning."

Her psychiatrist claimed that Mary did so much writing in her career that she somehow projected it onto the wall, but Mary herself obviously believed in spirits, saying that she planned to have the house exorcised again. When asked if she were religious, Mary answered, "No, but if I had a religion it would be Catholic because they believe in the devil. That's something I'm hung up on."

If the spirits writing on the wall were indeed warning Mary Zakos, she didn't heed their message. Five years after the article appeared, she died at the age of forty-three in the same house where she had been born. By some accounts, her death was a suicide and the cause was an overdose and poisoning by a combination of drugs. After this tragedy, Eleanor Zakos moved into a nursing home, and her son Tom decided to sell the house, listing it with Missoula realtor Jim Olson.

"By this time, the place was really a mess, the worst I've ever seen," Jim told me. "There were piles of garbage everywhere, and lots of things needed repair. But I wish I had haunted houses on the market every day, because I got more action on the Zakos house—sometimes fifteen or twenty calls a day—than on any other property before or since. Of course, lots of people weren't serious about buying—they just wanted to see a haunted house or to communicate with the spirits."

On September 7, 1986, the *Missoulian* ran a front-page story about Jim's trying to sell "the city's quintessential haunted house." Titled "FOR SALE: spirited Victorian charmer," the article by Mea Andrews claimed that three psychics had been among the throng of people who looked at the house. One of them claimed that the spirits were friendly but that anyone who bought the house would have to make peace with them because they were definitely going to stay.

One prospective buyer, Carol Togtmar, became so intrigued that she interviewed Eleanor Zakos and did other research on the history of the house. She also explored the dwelling with a mystic who claimed to sense "perverted violence" and "sex" there, even though Togtmar had told him nothing of Mary Zakos's penchant for titillating horror stories. Togtmar also said that the mystic had gotten a strong impression that the home's original ghostly inhabitant was an old woman who had died there.

"She had been treated badly by her family," Togtmar was quoted as saying in the article. "When she died she wasn't found for a little while. She had such hatred . . . she left her spirit behind." The mystic claimed that other spirits had moved into the house too, attracted by the negative energy.

Togtmar's research led her to wonder whether the mistreated old woman could have been the mother or wife of Frederick C. Scheuch, the man who built the house in 1902. He was a professor of languages and mechanical engineering and a three-time interim president at the University of Montana. The research had also uncovered the fact that Jimmie Scheuch, the professor's wife, died in the house on April 16, 1935, succumbing to a heart attack that occurred during a bout with the flu. The *Missoulian* article doesn't speculate on the cause of the screams heard by the Zakos family, but it seems plausible that if the mystic's "vibrations" were correct, the shrieks might have been the ghostly echoes of a woman who was abused during her lifetime.

The *Missoulian* noted an eerie coincidence Jim Olson experienced at the time he was trying to sell the Zakos house. He was showing a house in east Missoula when he noticed a stack of old yellowing newspapers in the garage. He casually picked up the one that happened to be on top and noticed its date, August 7, 1949. He scanned the page and there, on the right-hand side, was the wedding announcement of Alice Lindborg to Tom Zakos—the owner of the house on Fifth Street.

Several years have passed since the Zakos family sold their home, and at this writing the dwelling is still in a dilapidated condition. Vandals, not ghosts, have caused the greatest number of problems in recent years, and the current owners are understandably tired of all the publicity about a house that doesn't seem to be haunted anymore. They are planning to renovate the structure and to live there themselves; by making it a happy place, perhaps they'll be successful in "exorcising" it once and for all from the negative influences of its past.

Six
· · · · ·

Montana's Haunted Mines

Genuine ghost stories from Montana's mines are like veins of gold, silver, and copper running below the earth's surface—you know they're there, but they're hard to find, and, often, attempts to excavate them leave you feeling that you've barely scratched the surface.

One problem with collecting supernatural lore from Montana's mines is that so many of the best-known tales are either outright hoaxes or simple cases of mistaking one thing for another. What is probably the state's most famous spook story is that of the so-called "Centerville ghost," which was admitted to be a hoax—but not until thirty years after newspaper accounts created mass hysteria among the residents of Centerville and Butte.

For almost two weeks in March 1901, the *Anaconda Standard* scared readers silly with articles about the black-shrouded apparition that reportedly stalked the streets of Centerville at night. According to an article on March 6, the strange creature first appeared to two men who initially believed it to be a woman because of its long flowing robes. But then it stepped in front of them, throwing back its veil to disclose a hideous face.

"For a moment we were transfixed in amazement," the witnesses were quoted as saying, "for the features, whether male or female, being or spirit, were most horribly distorted, marked, and were illuminated by blue streaks of sulphur." Before the witnesses could run away, the apparition screamed in agony and fled down some railroad tracks.

A series of stories followed, fueling the fires of macabre gossip until it seemed that half the population of Centerville had tangled with the ghost. One miner even sent a letter to the editor describing his encounter with the ghastly being on the tracks up Dublin Gulch.

"I could not take my eyes from it," the letter explained, "and I know that it was glaring at me beneath the folds of the long black veil which covered its face. Raising one arm above its head I followed the movement. In the hand was a grinning skull. With the other hand it threw back the veil, revealing the most horrible looking countenance I have ever looked upon . . . Around the face hovered an unearthly blue light quite different from that produced by phosphorous."

During the height of "ghost fever," armed vigilantes lay in wait for the spook near its usual haunt at the Mountain Con Mine, and several nights later two very drunk would-be assassins shot the apparition on the railroad tracks near a bridge on Main Street. Naturally, the bullets, later revealed to be blanks, were reported to pass right through the phantom's body without doing any harm.

During its eleven-day reign of terror, the Centerville ghost bloodied the face of one young man and chased another so that he fell and skinned his nose; the spook kidnapped a young woman as she left a streetcar, bound her face with strips of black cloth, and tied her to a post near some railroad tracks on Montana Street. Then, for reasons known only to the ghost, it untied its victim, carried her farther up the street, and tied her to another post before lighting a cigarette, smoking it, and disappearing up some stairs near a saloon. The abandoned woman reportedly almost froze to death before being discovered at 4:00 A.M. by a blacksmith.

Various theories regarding the specter's identity were put forward, but none were conclusive. An article on St. Patrick's Day ended the series on the Centerville ghost, and the tone should have tipped off readers that the whole episode had been fabricated.

"The ghost has worked the game well," the writer of the piece remarked. "He has surely afforded the populace some fun if he has whitened the hairs of the few to whom he appeared with distressing suddenness. He has probably helped in rearing the children of Centerville in the right path, for since his appearance the youngsters have gone to bed with the chickens and displayed a willingness to do so that was pleasing to parents.

"It is a safe guess that the ghost will not boast of his pranks until the fever has blown over," the story continued. "When someone boasts over the bar that he played ghost his hearers can put it down to booze. It will take the ghost some months to outlive the realization that playing ghost came mighty near making a ghost out of him."

And then the article revealed that the supernatural troublemaker was no more: "So much for the ghost; for the ghost is dead."

The story of the Centerville phantom rested in peace for almost thirty years until local author Joe Duffy confessed that he and two newspaper reporters had concocted the wild tales during a slow news day, at first making up false accounts by imaginary witnesses and then perpetuating the hoax by printing the stories of imaginative readers who claimed that they, too, had seen the apparition.

Exaggerated versions of what appeared originally in the *Anaconda Standard* were published in the book *Copper Camp* in the 1930s and in a 1978 issue of *True West*. An article by Peter Chapin, "The ghost that Haunted Centerville," was published on November 3, 1979, in the *Montana Standard*, and this piece chronicles the story as it evolved and points out some of the discrepancies between the original news accounts and the later, even more fanciful, versions.

The Centerville ghost may be the best-known, but it is not the first hoax of a supernatural kind to find its way into Montana newspapers. Before the turn of the century, reporter "Silver Dick" Butler, nicknamed for the color of his hair, contrived a tale about a ghost who haunted the abandoned hoist of the Odin Mine in Dublin Gulch. This hoax is described in an article in an unidentified paper published on February 13, 1922, now collected in the Montana Newspaper Association Inserts. Titled "Ghost Stories of Early Day Butte and How Imaginative Reporter Started Them," the piece explains that on an uneventful day Butler's boss instructed him to "fake something—a ghost story if nothing else."

The reporter chose Dublin Gulch as the setting for his tale because he counted on frightening the Irish immigrants living there. Because Irish folklore was filled with legends of all kinds of supernatural creatures, Butler decided to make the dwellers of the gulch feel right at home by giving them their very own ghost story.

Unfortunately, the article doesn't give any details about the eerie tale Butler dreamed up except to say that it "followed the lines approved of by the best spook writers of that period." The reporter could hardly wait to find out how well his story had been received, so just a few hours after the evening paper was delivered he walked to the gulch to see for himself. One miner's residence was very close to the supposedly haunted hoist, and from its doorway Butler was gratified to hear a woman calling to her child: "Patsy, Patsy! Come in here or the ghost'll get ye."

The smug reporter strolled along, coming to a cottage where a young man appeared to be leaving for a night on the town. From the porch, a woman cried out, "Now Micky dear, don't stay out late, for I'll be worrying wid that ghost in the gulch."

Butler was delighted to see how well his scary tale had caught on. He continued walking until he reached a saloon; he entered it and strode up to the bar, where several husky Irish men were talking. They had obviously been discussing the ghost story, for the largest one turned to the reporter, shook his fist, and shouted, "I'd give tin dollars to lay me hands on the durty skunk that put that piece in the paper." Needless to say, "Silver Dick" Butler published no follow-up story in the next day's edition.

In addition to the mining-related ghost stories fabricated by reporters, there were others that arose from simple mistakes in perception. A story that appeared first in the *Daily Intermountain* on February 16, 1901, and then reappeared in an undated "Notes from the Archives" column by John Hughes, concerns the "ghost of the Wharton Mansion," then at 319 North Montana. Jesse R. Wharton, referred to as "the most popular man in Butte," explained that shortly after he and his wife married and moved into the house in March 1886, they heard footsteps downstairs one night just as the clock struck midnight. The footsteps sounded as if they were moving from the front parlor to the dining room. Afraid that a burglar was in the house, the Whartons armed themselves and rushed downstairs. But no one was there, and there were no signs of forced entry.

The next night at midnight they heard the footsteps again, and Wharton seized a log and threw it out of an upstairs window, hoping it would strike the trespasser as he left through the kitchen door. But, once again, after a thorough search, there was no sign of an intruder.

The Whartons looked for the presence of rats the next day and found none. But they continued to hear the phantom footsteps, always at the stroke of midnight. One night the couple sat together downstairs in the dark, waiting for the noises to come again. They did, only this time they seemed to be upstairs.

The following night, Mrs. Wharton waited on the upper floor and her husband remained downstairs in the living room. Once again, the clock struck midnight and the ghostly footsteps sounded, but both of the Whartons heard them on the floor opposite to where they were stationed.

The young couple became increasingly anxious to find a solution to their problem. Thinking he might learn more by leaving the house one night, Mr. Wharton sat out on the front steps; his wife stayed indoors. At the stroke of midnight the mystery was finally solved.

What made the sound of footsteps in the house? "The midnight blasts in the Gagnon [mine], going off promptly as they should have done," Jesse Wharton explained in the *Intermountain* article. "One after another made it sound as if [a person were] going from one room to another. Best imitation of the real article I ever saw, or rather heard."

Then he noted that the reporter was disappointed. "Why?" Mr. Wharton asked. "I call it a pretty good ghost story myself."

An even better mining-related ghost story, also based on faulty perceptions, was reported in the *Jordan Gazette* on December 13, 1920. The article by Frank Lovell, " 'Gambler's Ghost' Had Butte's Nerves Jumping; Amateur Sleuth Located Spook," tells the story of an apparently disembodied voice that captured the imagination of the public in the autumn of 1917.

The strange sequence of events began in Julius Fried's East Broadway cigar store when a porter came running from the basement (which was actually part of an old mine shaft abandoned twenty years before) in terror, yelling that he'd heard a ghost pleading, "Let me out." The clerk tried to reassure the porter that the sounds must have come from a sign painter who had a studio there. The clerk went to the basement to investigate both the sign painter's premises and some other small rooms that had originally been built as gambling dens. Everything was empty, but the clerk also heard the voice wailing, "Let me out," and it seemed to be right next to him.

"Wha-a-t do you want?" the clerk stammered, and the voice repeated its demand, except that now it seemed to be coming from the low-hanging ceiling. The clerk crashed into a box as he hurried to get out of the basement, and the voice screamed again, "Let me out! Let me out!"

Several brave employees then banded together to search every corner of the basement, and one called out, "Ghost, where are you?" Instantly the reply came, as if the voice were right next to the men. "I'm here," it said. "Let me out."

The searchers asked the question repeatedly and each time the voice seemed to answer from a different place—from the ceiling, from beneath their feet, from far down in the shaft, from right inside their own ears. In spite of the gooseflesh creeping up their spines, the men continued their investigation but found no cause for the mysterious voice.

When the story appeared in the newspaper, citizens advanced all kinds of theories. Perhaps the voice came from a kidnap victim or from a miner who had lost his way in the deserted diggings. The best story, however, came from an oldtimer who remembered that a gambler had been murdered in one of the old dens twenty years ago that week.

The newspaper followed up this angle by interviewing a medium who communed with the gambler's spirit. The message of the slain man to the Butte populace was unclear, but the spirit kept referring to a wound in his head. The oldtimer confirmed that that was indeed where the gambler had been shot.

Employees led another expedition to the basement, and this time they followed the shaft all the way to the old engine station, where they came to a "jumping-off place" and could go no farther. Along the way they kept calling out, "Where are you?" and the voice never failed to respond, each time coming from a different direction.

The mystery was solved only when the leader of the expedition drew a rough diagram of the old mine, the cigar store, and the buildings on both sides of the street. After studying the diagram, the searchers realized that the city hall, with the city jail beneath it, was directly opposite the cigar store. The northern end of the jail and the southern end of the mine shaft were opposite each other, separated by the width of the street. The "ghost" turned out to be a drunken prisoner in the jail who greeted every sound he heard with a plaintive "Let me out." His voice was conveyed along a fracture in the rock beneath the street, and the mine shaft amplified the sounds and bounced them around so that they seemed to be coming first from one place and then from another.

An undated column called "Echoes from the Distant Past" describes in jarring prose the antics of another spook who might also have been made of flesh and blood. The events described below occurred near Butte in July 1902:

> There is a ghost in the Highlands, according to the white population which consists of three men who have been residents of the gulch since 1866. This Highland ghost differs from any other phantom. It makes its presence known by singing and shouting from the top of some old shack or from the top of a pile of rock. Boyle Ransom, who lives over the hill in Moose Gulch came to Butte yesterday. He says: "The ghost is robed in white. He has long flowing white hair. He has a long white beard which he carries over his arm when he runs which is frequently. He looks like a man but has the voice of a woman. Last night he, she or it, roared out several verses of 'The Star Spangled Banner.' Johnny Cann, the oldest man in Highland gulch popped out and banged away with his trusty rifle. Johnny is no amateur with a gun. Whether he hit it or not depends on whether it is a human or a spirit; anyway it disappeared in the direction of Horse gulch. During the past 10 years the Highlands have supported a small colony of Chinese who have kept the water muddy by working over old ground and taking out a few dollars every summer. This summer there are only

about half a dozen Orientals left and these with the three white men already mentioned constitute the population of the camp. The Chinese today are not even making Chinese wages. The white men manage to take out enough gold, however, to keep them trying. The ghost is scaring the Chinese stiff. The white miners seem to stand up under the strain of having a supernatural visitor with the usual Caucasian stoicism. Once Highland City numbered 150 houses. Today there are only two houses remain [sic] and they are merely shacks."

The Chinese occupy them, the white miners' cabins are outside the city district. Highlands will last as long as these three white men live, it is anticipated. The Chinese population will remain as long as a color can be washed out of the old diggings—unless the ghost should wreck their nervous systems.

That Boyle Ransom may have been imbibing spirits of the liquid variety when he "saw" the Highlands ghost and that this extremely peculiar spook was invented solely for the purpose of scaring off the Chinese miners both seem likely possibilities, especially when we consider the racism inherent in the piece and in the historical period itself.

Another unlikely ghost near Butte was featured in an Associated Press story on September 6, 1965. In this report, a group of twenty boys claimed to have seen a "misty, white figure with big red eyes" near the Orphan Girl Mine. No more details of this sighting are given, but the article explains that, years before, reports of a headless miner's ghost were common and that he "was seen wandering round the mines with a candle in his hand, looking for his head."

Al Hooper, of the World Mining Museum in Butte, remembers hearing tales of this headless specter, who terrorized the men of the West Colusa Mine. "A friend of mine who died years ago swore that a lot of men believed the story to be true," Al said. "This was back sometime between 1910 and 1920. Apparently some miners had seen a man running up the drift carrying his head under his arm; there was so much talk about it that quite a few men actually quit their jobs. Others would come to the level where the ghost was seen and they'd start imagining things. After a while, so few men were willing to work on that level that the management put out a sign saying that anyone caught talking about the headless ghost would be discharged."

Al's friend also told him a story that took place at the Mountain View Mine around the same time. "Miners often eat with their lunch buckets placed in front of them on a long plank called a lagging," Al explained. "The lagging lies across a block to make a kind of table so the miner can stretch his legs to be more comfortable while he eats. One time during the graveyard shift, several miners had just finished eating and the conversation was beginning to wind down when all of a sudden they heard footsteps coming down the ladder from the stope above them.

"Nobody could figure out who would be climbing down during the lunch hour, so they waited to see who it was and what he wanted," Al continued. "The lights on their level weren't very good, but they were bright enough to illuminate the opening so that anyone climbing down the ladder would be seen clearly. The miners kept watching, and they could all hear the footsteps coming closer and closer. They still didn't see anyone, and then the footsteps went right by them and on down the ladder to the level below. The guys never could figure out what was going on, but this experience sure scared them."

Al Hooper also recalled the spooky experience of three fellow miners during the reopening of the Granite Mountain shaft, the site of the largest metal mine disaster in U.S. history. On June 8, 1917, one hundred sixty-three miners were killed when a fire broke out just a few minutes before midnight. Many perished immediately in the blaze, and others died when deadly gas and smoke spread quickly through the mine. Although many men managed to escape and brave rescuers saved others, it still took three days for all the entombed bodies to be recovered.

The city of Butte took a long time to heal after the tragedy, and twenty-three years later, in 1940, the mine was reopened. Al Hooper was the hoist engineer at this time, working the graveyard shift on a beautiful moonlit night.

"I was standing right by the mine shaft when three men came up from underground," he explained. "Right away I could see that something was wrong. These were grown men, but they looked scared to death. One man said, 'There's somebody breathing down there.'

"I couldn't believe what I was hearing," Al said. "He told me again that they'd heard what sounded like someone breathing deeply. I told him that such a thing was impossible, that the disaster happened in 1917 and this was 1940—how could anybody still be alive down there?

"That's when one of the men looked solemnly at me and said, 'The spirit of someone could be.' All three of them looked so shaken that I didn't have the heart to say more, so I just walked away.

"I've thought about this incident over the years, and I've always wondered, because we were bringing ventilation in with us, if the wind had whistled around a piece of canvas or a board and made some sort of sound that fooled them," Al said. "But those three men were convinced that what they heard was the sound of someone breathing."

It's hard to believe that true stories of haunted mines are so scarce in Montana, especially because many of the state's best-known fictional tales concern the same subject. Of course, no one yet understands why some events apparently have psychic repercussions while others don't, but I suspect there are hundreds of spooky, true yarns from Montana's mines—someone just needs to know how to excavate them.

Seven

The Tragedy of Big Hole Battlefield

Some events in human history are so heartbreaking that they can't help but leave strong psychic impressions on the places where they occur. One such event is a tragic battle that should never have been fought, involving Colonel John Gibbon's 7th U.S. Infantry and a band of Nez Perce at the Big Hole Valley in southwestern Montana.

To understand the significance of what happened in those early morning hours of August 9, 1877, we must first know something of the history of the Nez Perce themselves, a semi-nomadic, peaceful people whose traditional homeland was the area where Oregon, Washington, and Idaho meet. The Nez Perce had a long history of friendship with white settlers, and in a treaty of 1855 this group of Native Americans agreed to give up a portion of their holdings and move to a reservation. The deal was acceptable to most of them because the reservation included much of the land that had belonged to their ancestors. The treaty also specified that non-Indians could live there only with the Indians' consent.

Settlers and miners wanting more of the Nez Perce lands forced a new treaty in 1863, which diminished the reservation to a fourth of its original size. The chiefs whose lands fell within the area of the reduced reservation agreed to the new treaty, but fully a third of the Nez Perce lived in areas outside its shrinking boundaries, and they refused even to participate in the talks. These tribal members, referred to from that time on as the "non-treaty" Nez Perce, also claimed that because they had never recognized a leader who could speak for the entire tribe, no one had the right to sign an agreement in their place.

The non-treaty group continued to live on their land until 1877, when the Indian Bureau ordered them to move to the small reservation in western Idaho Territory. At first they refused, so General O. O. Howard issued an ultimatum that all Nez Perce were to be on the reservation within thirty days. Several non-treaty leaders, including Chief Joseph, explained that a month was not long enough for the eight hundred people to gather up their animals and make the move; they asked to be allowed

On the shores of Washington State's Lake Chelan, Chief Joseph posed with an old foe, Colonel John Gibbon. When this picture was taken, in 1889, Gibbon had been promoted to general. *(Courtesy Smithsonian Institution; photo number 43,201)*

to wait until the autumn, when the Snake River would be lower and easier to cross. General Howard was unsympathetic, however, and reiterated his demand that they move to the reservation immediately.

Sadly, but with no other choice, the non-treaty Nez Perce began their arduous journey and were just short of their thirty-day deadline when they stopped to camp. Ironically, they were only a few miles from what would have been their new home.

They were not to join their fellow Nez Perce after all, for on June 15, three young warriors in the band killed four white settlers after accusing them of cheating or killing older members of their tribe. The rest of the non-treaty Nez Perce knew that the entire band would be pursued and punished by the U.S. Army, so to avoid further conflict most of them retreated south to White Bird Canyon. General Howard's forces met up with them there and suffered many casualties but were unable to vanquish the small group of Indians. The next month, the army and the Nez Perce clashed again with no decisive victory on either side.

The non-treaty Nez Perce realized that their only hope for peace was to move out of Idaho Territory altogether and to join the Crow tribe farther east in Montana Territory. Under the leadership of Chief Looking Glass, the band made the weary trek to the Crow lands, and on August 7 they reached the Big Hole Valley.

Once there, they believed themselves to be out of danger at last, and they spent their first day of freedom setting up tipis, singing, dancing, and celebrating. Life would be good again, and Chief Looking Glass did not feel the need to post guards to watch over the encampment at night.

Although the Nez Perce didn't realize it, the threat from General Howard had been replaced by one from Colonel John Gibbon. He and the one hundred and eighty-two men in his 7th U.S. Infantry discovered the Indian camp on the afternoon of August 8 and planned to attack right after dawn the next morning. By 2:00 A.M., the soldiers were in place behind a skirmish line along the bank of the Big Hole River, waiting for dawn to break.

Fate intervened again, making the tragedy even worse than it would have been if the soldiers had waited until daylight to fire on the little village. Shortly before dawn, a Nez Perce man left the encampment to check the horses grazing on the slopes behind where Gibbon's troops were hiding. When the unsuspecting fellow walked straight into the skirmish line he was shot and killed instantly.

The all-out attack on the sleeping village began. It was still dark, and the soldiers could barely see what, or whom, they were shooting as they crossed the riverbank firing their guns.

Barely awake, the Nez Perce ventured from their tipis to see what was happening, and many were killed immediately, before they could fully regain consciousness. Young warriors were shot down before they could think of defending themselves, and the pleas of the elderly for mercy were ignored as they, too, were massacred. Young women tried in vain to shield their terrified infants, but both mother and child were struck down without pity. Older children clung horrified to the bodies of their dead parents, and these innocents, too, were slaughtered.

Amid the carnage of the camp, a few of the more alert Indians managed to find good sniping positions and returned the soldiers' fire with deadly accuracy. Incredibly, the Nez Perce were eventually able to force the soldiers back across the Big Hole River, where they held them hostage all that day and the next. While the warriors had the soldiers under siege, Chief Joseph rounded up what was left of his people and took them south. The Nez Perce had won the battle, at least in a military sense, but their victory was meaningless.

Approximately forty women, children, and old people, as well as about thirty warriors, had been killed in the early morning raid. And perhaps even more bitter was the realization, at last, that no matter where they went or what they did, the army would hunt them down and force them onto the reservation. Their way of life was gone forever.

Any occurrence as brutal as the massacre of the sleeping village is bound to produce psychic echoes that linger long after the event itself is over. Adding to the horror of the death scene was a tribe of Shoshone Bannock who came along after the fight to open up the Nez Perce graves, scalping and mutilating the corpses.

Is it any wonder that visitors to the Big Hole National Battlefield still experience the presence of the dead more than one hundred fifteen years after they were killed?

"It happens almost every summer," said park ranger Wilfred Half-moon, himself a Nez Perce who grew up hearing his parents' stories about the raid and later researched the subject on his own. "Tourists often cry when they visit the battlefield, and they say they can feel the spirits of the dead all around them."

Wilfred feels especially close to those spirits himself, because his great-grandfather was one of those killed. And like many other visitors to the site, Wilfred has often prayed for the souls of all who lost their lives that day, especially the children.

"Many of the Nez Perce people still come back here and leave their medicine bundles on the battlefield," he explained. "Sometimes they leave eagle feathers or little bells. This space has been very, very sacred ground for my people through the years."

For this reason, Wilfred explained, he was at first hesitant to share his own most unusual experience at the site. But because now his role as a park ranger is to help "interpret" the battlefield for the public, he has decided that what happened to him may help others to comprehend more fully the tragedy that occurred there.

"In the late 1960s, when I was about seventeen, my friend Harry and I traveled to the battlefield with a church group," Wilfred began. "I told Harry that we ought to camp down below where the fighting had been, and at first he didn't want to, although I eventually talked him into it. Nobody else wanted to join us because they were too scared.

"We took our sleeping bags down there, made a little fire, and just enjoyed camping out by a little stream," Wilfred continued. "Soon it got dark and everything was quiet all around us. But later on in the night we began hearing something we couldn't believe.

"We heard the sounds of lots of people moving around and we began to get really scared. We jumped up, looked at each other, and wondered what we should do. We climbed up on top of a hillside where the horse pasture was located and looked down. We couldn't see anything, but we heard the sounds of people running through the water.

"Fascinated but very frightened, we stayed there, and later we began hearing women crying, babies squalling, and then a terrible screaming. The sounds below us were very, very loud, but we could see that there was no one down there. Those were noises I never wanted to hear again— they were so pitiful. We continued listening for a while, and the sobbing of the women made us sad. Finally, we just had to leave, so we walked out of there.

"Even today I can still feel the presence of those people," Wilfred admitted, "but I don't hear the sounds much anymore, not like I used to. Most of the Nez Perce people don't like talking about such things, but I know that others have had the same experience."

When Wilfred told me his story in December 1991, the Nez Perce were planning to build a monument for those killed in the battle, especially the women and children. Such a remembrance is long overdue, even though nothing that anyone does now can alter the events of more than one hundred years ago. But perhaps any tribute to the dead serves its highest purpose when it reminds us, the living, that we are all sisters and brothers in the same human family.

Eight

The Haunting of the Montana State University Theater

Wherever there are theaters, there are likely to be ghosts, and current theories about psychic phenomena may help to explain why. Parapsychologists know that whatever else so-called "supernatural" occurrences may be, they are definitely manifestations of energy. This energy may come from disembodied spirits or merely from residual emotions that somehow become recorded on the physical environment, to be "played back" under conditions not yet fully understood.

Is it so hard to believe, then, that the spirits of actors, directors, or others who loved the stage during their lives might choose to linger there after death? Or that all the emotional intensity produced by actors performing and audiences responding might be psychically imprinted onto the very walls or the floor and then somehow released?

Whatever theater ghosts are, Montana has more than its share. And of all the theaters in the entire state, none has more tragic reason to be haunted than the one at Montana State University (MSU) in Bozeman.

When Chris McLaren came to MSU in the mid-1970s, she heard rumors that the theater had a ghost. She never took the stories seriously, however, until one night when she and another student stayed late to rehearse.

"Everybody had gone home except for the two of us," she remembered, "and because all the doors were locked on the outside, no one else should have had access to the building. Yet, while we were trying to concentrate on our scene, we kept hearing the sound of someone walking in the shop area behind the stage.

"There were two staircases leading from this part of the theater to the rooms downstairs," Chris explained, "and we distinctly heard footsteps going up and down the metal spiral staircase. Each time we heard the walking sounds, we went to see who was there, but we never found anyone. We even went downstairs to check the rooms below, but they, too,

An early photograph of the Montana State University Theater building, visible to the left of the Student Union. The tragic death of a theater director is believed responsible for many supernatural occurrences here. *(Courtesy Montana State University Archives)*

were empty. The sounds of the footsteps occurred so many times that we got a little spooked. Finally, we decided to leave."

What happened next has remained vivid in Chris's memory, and it definitely made her a believer in ghosts. "Before leaving, we were supposed to turn off all the lights and make sure the doors were locked behind us," she recalled. "But as we looked up from the stage, we saw a man in the sound booth. We couldn't imagine who he was or why he was there, but because we didn't want to lock anyone in for the night we went up to check.

"When we got there, the sound booth was empty," Chris said. "That seemed odd, but what was even more unsettling was coming back down again and seeing the same man in the same place—he hadn't moved an inch. I had never seen him before and I'll never forget what he looked like. His hair was graying and he had a beard, perhaps a goatee. He was also wearing a light-colored suit.

"Besides the fact that the sound booth was empty when we checked it," Chris said, "another problem was that even if someone had been in there, it wouldn't have been possible to see him at the window as we did. A control board was placed right against the glass, leaving such a small space that no human being could have fit there.

"After seeing the man for the second time, we just wanted to get out of that place—fast! We left without turning off one bank of lights, because there was no way we were going to walk all the way from the stage to the door in the dark. When we came back the next morning everybody asked why we'd left the lights on. We explained what had happened and one of the professors said, 'I think we'd better tell you something.'"

Chris and her friend were shaken by the bizarre and tragic tale that unfolded. About two years before Chris arrived at MSU, a man named Jon Schmidt (a pseudonym) had been director of the theater program. Brilliant and talented, he was well known and very influential in Montana dramatic circles. On one occasion he was walking down the metal spiral staircase behind the stage when he slipped on the treacherous steps and fell all the way to the bottom. The accident left him with a massive concussion.

Brain injuries of this kind sometimes create deep depressions and dramatic mood swings and, unfortunately, Jon Schmidt suffered from both. For about two weeks following the accident he grew more and more despondent. On opening night of a production, in his office right next to the sound booth, he shot himself with a prop pistol. His body was found shortly afterward by members of the sound crew.

"After telling us about how the poor fellow died, the professors asked if we'd gotten a good look at the man who had been up in the sound booth the night before," Chris continued. "I said that I had and then described him. When I finished, they looked at each other and said, 'You've just described Jon Schmidt.'

"I don't recall ever seeing any pictures of him," Chris said, "before or after we had our strange experience, and the professors were satisfied that there was probably no way we could have known what the former director looked like."

After the suicide, stories surfaced about a bloodstain marking the exact spot where Schmidt met his death. Gerry Roe, now at the drama department at Rocky Mountain College in Billings, worked at MSU from 1981 to 1987, and he inherited Schmidt's office.

"I'd heard about the suicide, of course, but at the time I had no idea that someday I would work at MSU," he explained. "When I first got there, Joel Jahnke, who is still director of the theater department, pointed out the stain to me. There's not much to it and I didn't think it would bother me. Joel continued showing me around, and a little while later I walked back around my desk and saw red spots on the floor. I totally freaked out—until I realized that Joel's little kid had drawn them there with a magic marker.

"Except for this rather shaky start, I didn't mind being in the office for the first six months," Gerry said. "But then, for some reason, it started getting to me. I couldn't stand to be alone in that room or even in the building late at night. And whenever I saw myself in the double-glass windows overlooking the theater, I was startled by my own reflection.

"I was okay if someone was with me, but that wasn't always possible. I began going into the building at six o'clock in the morning to get my work done, and nothing ever bothered me then.

"The whole time I was there, I heard a lot of talk about people experiencing strange phenomena," Gerry continued. "One night I was back in the shop area getting ready to leave the theater when I saw what seemed to be a backlighted silhouette of a man. I had just checked the doors about ten minutes before and I didn't see how it was logistically possible for anyone to have gotten in since then. I don't know if I saw a ghost or what, but I was so frightened that I took off down those curved stairs and flew out some doors into the alley. I've thought about this experience a lot since then, and I just don't know how a flesh-and-blood human being could have gotten into the building that night."

Although the tragic story of Jon Schmidt certainly seems reason enough for the MSU theater to be haunted, some accounts of ghostly phenomena there actually precede his death and point to the presence of another entity. Steve Wing, now production coordinator for drama at the University of Montana in Missoula, was working in the MSU theater in the fall of 1970, and he remembers a very strange experience that occurred late one night.

"The greenroom also doubled as a performing space, and we were doing a show there at that time," Steve explained. "We were using a piece of electronic equipment called a light organ, which casts different patterns on a plastic screen to match various sounds. The dress rehearsal had ended several hours earlier, and everything had been unplugged. A woman and I came up out of the costume shop to take a break, and we were very shocked to see the light organ come on and start pulsing. The woman stood there and watched it while I ran down to get the other people in the costume shop. When I returned with them, the thing was still pulsing.

"We double-checked the light organ, and it was definitely unplugged," Steve insisted. "There was no obvious source of electricity going into it, and we wondered if the power had somehow built up so that the capacitors were just at that time releasing it. An electrician assured us that such a thing wasn't possible after the light organ had been shut off for a long time. We never could figure out what caused the strange pulsing."

If a spirit was to blame for this odd manifestation, it obviously wasn't Schmidt's, because this incident occurred four years before his death. And although no one knows for sure how many ghostly presences are wreaking havoc at the theater, it appears that at least one of them is female.

Former student Bill Koch heard rumors that a woman had hanged herself in the ballroom of the Student Union Building, now called the Strand Student Union, in an area near what became the light room of the theater. I checked with Mildred Leigh, director of the student union from 1940 to 1968. She had never heard the rumor, and she felt sure that if such a thing had happened she would have known about it. She in turn checked with some other early-day employees of the union, and none of them believed that the story had any basis in fact.

Two sightings of an apparition are especially interesting in light of the rumor, however. Approximately five years ago, a costume student was on stage when she saw a woman standing in the house. Before the specter disappeared, the student noticed that she was clad in an evening dress from the style of the late 1920s or early 1930s. A month or two later, the student saw the apparition again, wearing the same clothing and standing in the same spot. It is intriguing to speculate whether this woman was the one reputed to have hanged herself (if, in fact, such an event ever occurred). And although it's unlikely that anyone would wear an evening gown to commit such a gruesome act, it's interesting nevertheless that a phantom dressed to go to a dance should appear near the site of the old ballroom.

Regardless of the truth of the rumor, other people have also reported eerie phenomena involving a phantom woman. A. J. Kalanick, now a full-time actor, encountered, in 1986, what he is sure was a female ghost. "I walked into the theater by myself, calling out the name of an actress with whom I was to rehearse a scene," he replied. "The theater was totally dark except for the red lights shining from a boom box stereo the actress had left on the stage. I kept calling out her name and getting no response. I walked down the aisle, and as I got to the edge of the stage I heard footsteps coming off the stairs toward me. I called the actress's name again and got no answer, but suddenly I felt some fabric brush over my arm. Thinking the actress was there after all, I reached out to grab her, and there was only empty space. I called her name again and felt a hand run down my arm, but still no one was there.

"At that point, I turned and ran like crazy out of the theater and bumped into the actress in the hall. She said I looked like I'd seen a ghost, and I told her that at least I'd touched one. Together we went back into the theater and turned on the lights. I told her that earlier the lights from her boom box had been on. "'You couldn't have seen them,' she said. 'The batteries gave out and that's why I left, to get new ones at the bookstore.'

"There's no way that the lights on her stereo could have been on, and yet they were," A. J. insisted. "And I'm not sure whose hand and arm I felt, but they definitely seemed to belong to a woman.

"Another time, during a show Gerry Roe was directing, I was standing off on the side stage when I heard a woman scream. I turned to the stage manager and asked, 'Who the heck is that?' He didn't hear it, and she screamed again. I said, 'There—did you hear that?' But he hadn't, so obviously not everyone is sensitive to these phenomena."

Pamela Jamruszka-Mencher, who now teaches drama and speech at Red Rocks Community College in Lakewood, Colorado, is one of the few people who have actually seen the ghost of a woman who appears to be an actress. "I was the costumer, so I was often there very late at night," she explained. "My office was in the front of the theater, and when it was time to leave I walked through to the back, where I parked my car. The first time I saw the phantom on stage I thought she was a friend of mine. I hollered out, 'Hi, Lisa. Why are you still here?' Then the figure turned to me before it literally disappeared right before my eyes.

"She was blonde and looked about eighteen years old," Pam remembered. "I was standing in the house and she was about forty feet away, so it was hard to make out any facial features. The dress she was wearing was a costume of some sort, and the style was from the late eighteenth or early nineteenth century. I didn't hear her say anything, but she looked as if she were performing.

"When she disappeared right in front of me, I just knew I'd stayed up too late," Pam said, laughing. "But when I saw her the second time I became convinced that she wasn't just a figment of my imagination. On this occasion I had been one of the last to leave after the initiation ceremony for the theater fraternity. I was up above the stage on the catwalk when suddenly one of the lights came on and there was this same woman.

"This time I had the presence of mind enough not to holler," Pam said, "and I just stared at her. She was only about fifteen feet away, so I could observe her more closely. She was wearing the same dress I'd seen her in before, and her hair was piled on top of her head. She looked absolutely real and I wasn't frightened until, after about three seconds, she looked up at me and disappeared again. Now that I knew for sure I'd seen an apparition, I felt scared.

"After thinking about these two sightings over the years, I'm convinced that what I saw was the ghost of an actress playing a part," Pam explained. "There were some discrepancies in her costume, and it may well be that she was an actress in the 1940s playing someone from an earlier time."

Pam never got the feeling that the apparition was worried or upset, but a particularly eerie experience made her wonder if this spirit, or perhaps the spirit of Jon Schmidt, might have tried to contact her one evening.

"At one point I didn't have a place to live, so I ended up moving into the theater for a couple of weeks," Pam explained. "I stayed in a little area off to one side of the costume shop, under the stairs. We called this place the 'authentic room,' because it was here that we kept articles of actual clothing that were donated to be used as costumes. We had clothing from the nineteenth century, and this dry room helped to protect the fabrics.

"I made this place as comfortable as I could with a little bed, a lamp, and an aquarium with an angel fish," Pam continued. "One night I was up late studying and doing my laundry in the washing machine in the costume shop. I got up to change the clothes from the washer to the dryer, and when I came back to my room something felt strange to me. I had the feeling that someone had been there. I told myself I was just being silly, and I sat down in my chair and resumed studying.

"I always keep a notepad right next to the fish tank, and something made me look at it," Pam said. "Just a few minutes before the sheet on top had been clean, but now I saw some spidery handwriting, a mixture of cursive and block letters that looked like the scrawling of a drunk person. Stunned, I made out the words: 'Help me, somebody. Please help me.'

"'I'd like to help you,' I said, 'but I need to know who you are.'

"I tore the note off of the pad and examined it closely. And while I was doing that, a pencil lying on the table nearby began to roll, as if someone were about to pick it up.

"This was too much—I just couldn't handle any more," Pam confessed. "I know that nothing I did made the pencil move because I wasn't even touching the table when that happened. I was so scared that I ran out of the room and fled to a local restaurant where I sat up all night. I didn't come back until dawn.

"To this day I regret that I didn't have the courage to stay," Pam said, "because now that I'm older, I tend to think psychic phenomena are fairly harmless. But I hadn't figured that out when I was nineteen. As soon as I got back to my room I checked the note pad to see if someone had written a name or a message, but there was nothing.

"At the time, I thought the woman I'd seen on stage might have been the one trying to contact me, but it might have been Jon Schmidt. I didn't know him because I entered the theater program in 1974, just two days after his death; I remember what a hard time that was for everybody. And there were definitely unseen presences in the building."

Pam, who in addition to teaching now runs the Roving Stage Theater Company with her husband, has an interesting and plausible theory about why weird occurrences take place so often in theaters: "There's so much extreme emotion in a play, and I believe that sometimes it stays around," she explained. "Sensitive people might be aware of it and perhaps even add their own energies to it to cause some kind of physical manifestation. I think we can activate things that may be lying dormant. So I don't necessarily believe that all these things are attributable to spirits."

Probably the most common type of unexplained incident at the MSU theater is the disappearing and reappearing of objects. Costume and set designer Mary Alyce Hare will never forget one such experience that defied logic.

"I was alone in the building around one o'clock in the morning working on my first production at Montana State," she remembered. "It was called *Waltz of the Toreadors,* and it was to open in about a week and a half. At that time we had an oversized shoebox for storing all the buttons collected over the years, and I pulled it out and set it on the edge of our cutting table. Then I went around the corner and down the hall to the dressing room, where I picked up the smoking jacket that was to have the silver buttons.

"I returned to the costume shop and laid the jacket out on the table," Mary Alyce continued. "That's when I saw that the button box was no longer there.

"I'm a little nervous about being alone in the theater at night," she explained, "so I always make sure that all the doors to that area are locked. And on this particular night I knew I was the only person there. So even though I was sure I'd put that box on the table, I decided that I must have been mistaken and that I hadn't brought it out after all. I looked all over the shop, but I couldn't find the box anywhere. I finally got tired of searching and decided to look for it again the next day.

"When I came back, two seamstresses spent an hour with me trying to locate the button box, but we had no luck. Because this box had all the buttons we used for all the shows, we were really in a fix, and ended up having to buy buttons for the whole show.

"A few days after *Waltz of the Toreadors* opened, I started working on costumes for *The Elephant Man,*" Mary Alyce continued. "Again, it was late at night, I was by myself, and everything was locked up. This time I was going to cut fabric, and I cleared everything off of the table to make room for it. I went to pick up the material, just a few feet away, and when I came back the button box was on the table, just where I had last seen it two weeks before!

"This was a most bizarre occurrence because there was absolutely no one else in the building, and even if there had been, no one could have placed that box there without my seeing or hearing it. Remember that this is a big container full of buttons that click together noisily whenever the box is moved."

In addition to playing games with the buttons, the mischievous spirit has also trifled with the costumes. "We store these in a cage that used to be kept locked," Mary Alyce explained. "Several times I've taken garments out of the cage and placed them in the costume shop, only to have them disappear. Then I've found a substitute, and after the show opened I've discovered the original costume back inside the locked cage.

"The reverse has also happened, when I enlisted the entire crew to help me search for a particular costume that I knew existed. When we didn't find it, I locked the cage and went home. When I came in the next day, I found the costume we'd been looking for hanging in plain sight on the inside of the cage door. We like to joke that at least the ghost has good taste in the clothing it takes."

Mary Alyce says that most of the people who work in the costume shop believe that the presence is female. "A co-designer of mine who often works alone says that sometimes she feels someone walking behind her, and she catches a whiff of perfume. She turns to look, figuring that somebody has entered the door, but nobody's there."

Mary Alyce wryly recalls one incident in which she blamed the ghost for something it didn't do and then suffered the spirit's wrath as a consequence. "About seven or eight years ago, when we were doing 'Shakespeare in the Park' programs, I found a pair of shoes for an actor with an odd foot size," she said. "I'd taken them in to be repaired, and then I put them in the shop. A day or two before dress rehearsal I realized that the shoes were missing. By this time the actors were working and rehearsing outside, so it was possible that the shoes had gotten lost out there. I sent one of the actresses to look for them, but she had no luck.

"I was having a really bad day and I just assumed that the ghost had taken the shoes," Mary Alyce continued. "I was all by myself, and I walked into the shoe room and hollered an unprintable version of 'Okay, lady— we've had enough. I want those shoes back—now!'

"Then I walked out of the shoe room through the cage area and into the costume shop. In literally no more than two minutes all the sewing machines started to jam up, the iron began to spew water, and a seamstress who was doing some hand-sewing felt the needle snap in two in her hand. And she wasn't working on heavy fabric, either.

"At this point, I pulled aside the other designer and told her that I'd made a big mistake—I had infuriated the ghost by yelling at her. Then I ran back into the shoe room and apologized privately to the lady herself.

"Of course, all the problems stopped immediately," Mary Alyce said with a laugh, "and about ten minutes later an actress came waltzing through the door, saying, 'I found Henry's shoes. They were underneath something on the set.' So the ghost hadn't taken them after all."

Theater director Joel Jahnke admits that some of the peculiar goings-on might be attributed "to a bunch of rummy theater people running around at two in the morning." But he, too, has had an experience that defies explanation.

"I carried a board from a chair into the shop," he said. "I was looking for a clamp, and when I found it I took it out to the chair. Then I remembered that I'd set the board down in the tool room and I went back to get it. It wasn't there.

"Nobody had been anywhere near me in the shop or the tool room. I looked everywhere for that board, and later I had other people looking, too, but we never found it."

Still other unexplained phenomena have occurred at the MSU theater. In the middle of a performance, A. J. Kalanick and an actress heard someone walking directly behind them, from one side of the stage to the other, when it was obvious that no one was there. A. J. also recalls walking up the metal spiral staircase with two other men when the center pole seemed to "explode with light." He has never been able to explain what happened, but admitted, "We couldn't get off those stairs fast enough."

Another student, Stacey Gordon, often saw tiny blue flashing lights in the rafters of the greenroom, and she was on stage during a performance of *The House of Blue Leaves* when the sound of an explosion failed to take place as planned. The crew then slammed two doors to create the desired effect, but when the cast tried to go through the doors to the backstage area during intermission, they seemed to be glued shut. "They weren't just stuck—they absolutely wouldn't budge," Stacey recalled. "We had a football player in the cast who tried to pull one door open, but even he couldn't do it. Later, it opened easily, without being forced at all."

On another occasion, Stacey was playing one of the witches in the "unlucky play," *Macbeth*. She entered the stage during a performance and realized too late that she'd left her street shoes on. "I didn't want to turn around and walk off, so I tried to back into the hole where I'd come out," she explained. "I missed my mark, and at the same time a guy fell on me, hitting me in the head and knocking me unconscious.

"I honestly don't remember anything else, except that when I came to I found myself in the hole where I was supposed to be, safely underneath the stage," Stacey said. "I don't know how I got into it, because there's no way I could have crawled there. I think someone or something must have guided me."

Not everyone has felt so secure in the presence of the phantoms. Bill Koch, for example, was frightened by a strange sequence of events that took place after he received the Jon Schmidt theater scholarship in the early 1980s. "I never believed in ghosts before I went to MSU," he explained, "but I knew the legend that everyone receiving the scholarship would eventually encounter the spirit of the former director.

"I just laughed at that idea until late one night in July. I'd been working downstairs in the prop room, and when I went upstairs to lock everything up I felt as if ninety pairs of eyes were watching me. I stood on stage for a minute and called out, 'Hello, who's in here?'

"I didn't see how anyone could have gotten into the building because the front doors were locked and secured with safety bars. And yet I had the strangest feeling that I was not alone. As I stood on the stage, the area around me seemed to get darker, and when I went into the shop the window in the door looked as if it were fogged over, even though it was a sunny day. I had such a bad feeling that I backed down the stairwell and ran out of the building, not even bothering to lock the door behind me."

Bill's next weird experience took place the second week of August, when he was painting one of the makeup rooms. "Suddenly, I heard footsteps up above in the shop," he said. "I couldn't figure out who it was or how anyone could have gotten in because the front doors were locked, and I would have seen anyone who entered through the open back door.

"As I stood there listening for more footsteps, I heard the sound of the table saw starting up. That really annoyed me because I was in charge of the building, and no one else should have been in it. I started up the spiral staircase to check things out and I heard the band saw kick on, too.

"Now I was even more upset," Bill explained, "because it sounded as if someone were just playing around in the shop. Next the drill press came on and then the radial arm saw—that was the final straw! But the odd thing was that in spite of the fact that I heard all the saws running at once, I couldn't hear any wood being cut.

"From the top of the stairs I yelled for whoever was in the shop to get out, but I got no response. And just as I entered the shop door itself, all the saws suddenly shut off and everything was quiet again.

"There was no way that anyone could have turned off the saws and gotten out of the door that fast," Bill insisted. "In fact, the saws were all in different parts of the shop, so they couldn't even be turned off at the same time by just one person. And if anyone had run out, he would have had to pass right in front of me.

"Once again, I left the theater in a hurry—without locking up or even turning off the lights in the makeup room. I called the department head to tell him what I had done, and he told me that he understood completely because the same thing had happened to him."

The unexplained phenomena at the MSU theater seemed to intensify the next weekend with the opening of *Damn Yankees*, a play in which the protagonist sells his soul to the devil to become a baseball star. Half an hour before curtain, a huge paint rack that had been suspended from cables broke loose and crashed down onto the floor of the shop. Even though the area was full of people, the only person to hear the rack fall was the set director, who was also playing the part of the devil.

"The cable looked as if it had been sliced cleanly in two," Bill remembered. "If it had broken after wearing down, or even if someone had sawed it, it would have had a few frayed ends. But the smoothness of the cut was a total mystery."

Throughout the first act, more unsettling events plagued the cast and crew. First, a woman was frightened to see a noose hanging off the catwalk when it definitely had not been there five minutes earlier. Then the actors on stage clearly heard the explosion of a lighting instrument, but no shattered glass was ever found. And finally, the set director playing the devil tumbled from some steps into the first row of the audience, later claiming that he'd felt someone pulling the stairs right out from under him.

The spooky events weren't limited to the stage area, however. While the first act was still going on, Bill Koch took a break and went to the men's restroom. "As I was standing in there, I plainly heard a low unearthly laugh coming from the area right above my head, in the truss system only a foot under the ceiling," he said. "I ran out as soon as I could, and just as I reached the metal staircase a power surge in the stairwell made the lights pulsate weirdly. The area was so hot that it felt like a fire was burning, and when I got back to the stage I was so scared I could barely catch my breath.

"But for some reason, after intermission everything ran smoothly," Bill said. "I realized, though, that I'd definitely had my share of 'Jon Schmidt' experiences."

Bill was to have one more, however, when he heard the eerie laugh again several months later. He and two friends were sitting in the makeup room telling stories about the psychic phenomena at the theater. "Suddenly, that same hideous laugh came from the washroom below us," Bill said. "We immediately went to investigate, but no one was there. I was relieved, though, that someone besides me had finally heard it."

Bill continued to appear in productions after his graduation in 1985, and he recalls one evening when he had a feeling of impending danger while helping to hang lights. "I told the guy working with me that I thought something was going to happen, and that he should stay away from the electrical equipment for a while. And, sure enough, the light board shorted out. If he had continued working he would have been shocked."

That same night Bill was standing backstage in an old light booth, and he and the person next to him witnessed a free-floating transparent apparition that looked like a woman's skirt. The white wavy thing wafted through the air for a minute or so, then sped up to go between the watchers, forcing them out of the way before it disappeared. "I experienced the oddest sensation of hot and cold at the same time," Bill said, "and I have no idea what we saw.

"I didn't have any other unusual experiences at MSU, but one interesting coincidence did occur," Bill added. "I was working on my senior project at my home theater, the Blue Slipper in Livingston. The building was being remodeled, and a vinyl upholstery material had been put on the walls to cover them. There was a seam in the material, behind which people had stuck business cards. I peeled back the little lip of vinyl and pulled out the first one I found. Guess whose it was? Jon Schmidt's!"

Bill recalls one other experience linking him to the former theater director. At the time Schmidt died, there had been some wild talk and unsubstantiated speculation that someone had purposely caused his accident. The rumor was that some kind of oil used by the military might have been poured on the stairwell to make it even more slippery. "No one had ever been able to prove that oil had been poured on the stairs, and no container for it was ever found," Bill said. "But once when I was cleaning out the tool room, I found a bottle of this oil behind a built-in rack."

While practically no one now believes that Schmidt's fall was anything more than a tragic accident, almost everyone I talked to in the theater department has claimed to feel a presence, either Schmidt's or that of the unidentified woman phantom. Current director Joel Jahnke admits that he left the building one night after sensing that he was not alone, and two sound engineers almost walked out for the same reason, claiming that they had a bad case of "the willies."

If that's what they had, an epidemic of "the willies" must be making the rounds of the MSU drama department, where what goes on behind the scenes is just as dramatic as the performances themselves.

Nine

......

The Ghostly Procession

Some events are so outside what is commonly accepted as reality that our minds refuse to believe what our eyes and ears tell us. But anyone collecting stories of paranormal occurrences soon discovers that while these kinds of incidents may not be the norm, neither are they as rare as those experiencing them usually believe. And, paradoxically, the most convincing accounts of all generally come from those who are the least inclined to believe in supernatural phenomena.

Larry Bohne is one of these people. He considers himself to be logical and analytical, and that's why he has never before told anyone about a particularly unsettling incident that happened more than thirty years ago.

"Hunting big game with my father was the most important thing in my life when I was fourteen," Larry began his story. "Both a zeal for the sport and a love for my father compelled me to accompany him to the hills on a crisp October morning in 1961. We were waiting for mule deer beside a trickle of water called Dog Creek, in the shadow of the Crazy Mountains and about fifteen miles east of Livingston. Dog Creek is pleasantly lined by towering cottonwoods, thick patches of buck brush, and chokecherry bushes. The few hills in the area are covered with scrub pine, and beyond them the terrain becomes flat, with only sparse grass.

"We were having no luck in locating our game," Larry remembered, "and around eleven o'clock my father grew sleepy. He had gotten up at four that morning and he intended to nap for a while in our pickup. Being young and eager to bag a deer, I left him there and ventured forth on my own."

Larry reasoned that since there were no deer down near the creek, they might be sunning themselves higher up in the scrub pines. He began to climb out of the canyon, but the three or four inches of fresh snow made the steep walls slippery and hindered his progress.

"I finally got to the rim at the top of the canyon, looked out, and saw something I couldn't believe," Larry recalled. "I was more in awe of it than frightened, but right in front of me was a vast herd of buffalo

......

64

slowly making its way north. I was facing east, so the herd was moving off to my left. As the animals passed by, I began to notice a large number of people coming toward me as though they were following the retreating herd."

As the people drew nearer, Larry could see that they were Indians. "Some were walking and some were on horseback," he continued. "Most of them were men, but I did see some women and a few children, too. All of them were bundled up against the cold, and most of them were carrying their belongings on their backs.

"It was at this time that I noticed something particularly eerie about the scene unfolding in front of me," Larry explained. "There was no sound at all coming from either the buffalo or the Indians. I felt as though I were watching a movie instead of real beings, because even though I was standing in plain sight of all of them, neither the animals nor the humans passing before me gave any indication that they were aware of my presence. One small group of horsemen (four, as I recall) came within just ten or fifteen yards of me. I didn't get a good look at their faces, but I had the impression that the men were extremely weary and sad.

"The impact of what I was seeing suddenly hit me, and I turned around and ran all the way back down to the truck," Larry confessed. "I tried to relate what I had seen to my father, and he told me that I sounded like a babbling idiot. I finally convinced him to return to the spot with me, and on our way he tried his best to give a logical explanation for what I had seen. After all, my youthful imagination might have turned ranchers moving a herd of cattle into Indians with a herd of buffalo.

"My father's calm dissolved when we got to the rim of the canyon, however. The snow over which I had seen animals and people moving was smooth and unmarred, but in the far distance we both could plainly see the last of the phantom tribe walking over the horizon.

"The two of us walked without speaking for about half a mile in that direction, but we never again saw the eerie figures or any traces of them in the fresh untrampled snow. Only when we returned to the truck did my father speak again, cautioning me not to take the episode too seriously and admonishing me never to speak of it to anyone lest I be considered strange. Things like that were important to him, and I took him at his word. To the best of my knowledge, he never told anyone about our experience to the day he died in 1978, and this is the first time I have ever related it to anyone.

"I can only describe what I saw; I can't explain it," Larry admitted.

"Whether we witnessed a ghost tribe or became involved in a time warp, I can't say. But I can't dismiss the episode as imagination because we both saw it at the same time."

Would seeing the ghostly procession have been more or less unsettling for Larry if his father had not also seen it? If we set aside the unlikely possibility that at least two people can share a collective hallucination, it seems obvious that if another person sees what we see, we can both be more certain that whatever we are witnessing has some basis in reality. And for logical, rational people such as Larry Bohne (and for most of the rest of us as well), even the unknown is less frightening than the possibility that we're losing our sanity.

Ten
·····

Hannah Flagg, the Ghost of Niarada

Niarada, not far from Flathead Lake in the northwestern part of Montana, is so tiny that it isn't even included on some maps, and it is the site of one of the most intriguing ghost stories in the state. Maggie Plummer wrote about the little burg's premier phantom in an article titled "Spooky Niarada: Where things go 'bump' in the night" for the September/October 1987 issue of *Montana Magazine* (78–79). Since the story appeared, big changes have occurred in little Niarada. The Long Branch Bar and the post office have burned down, and many customers of both who told their spooky tales to Plummer have themselves passed from this world to the next.

A ranch hand we'll call Pete (a pseudonym) is still living, and even though he won't talk to strangers about his eerie experience, the story of his friendship with a winsome lady ghost is the one from which all other accounts have sprung, according to local resident Ann McDonald.

"I'm afraid that a lot of the stories in that *Montana Magazine* article were exaggerated," Ann said. "They made Hannah out to be a vengeful, wicked spirit who tried to suffocate people by holding pillows over their faces. I don't believe anything like that ever happened. For one thing, I'm pretty sure that Pete is the only person who actually encountered the ghost, and she never did anything mean to him. She was always very pleasant."

Ann said that while Pete was working for her brother-in-law and her late husband, Tom, he occasionally used to go out drinking at night. On his way back to the ranch he took less-traveled roads to avoid driving on the highway. If he felt too drowsy to make it home, he sometimes pulled off onto the shoulder near an old root cellar on the southern edge of Tom and Ann's ranch.

Pete told Tom about the dreams he had there, as often as two or three times a year, about a woman named Hannah and her two little girls. Hannah always looked the same: she wore a long skirt with an apron, and her hair was invariably pulled back into a bun. She was very

······

kind to Pete, and they enjoyed talking together while the two little girls, also wearing long old-fashioned dresses, played nearby.

Ann McDonald remembers Pete saying that once he tried to reach out for Hannah's hand, and she abruptly withdrew it, refusing to let him touch her. The McDonalds often joked with Pete about his mysterious woman friend, and everyone in the family referred to the area near the old root cellar as "Hannah's place."

For a long time the McDonalds refused to take their ranch hand's stories seriously. But to Pete himself, Hannah and her children seemed so lifelike that he began to believe they were real people, or at least real ghosts. Incredibly, Tom McDonald's chance encounter with a stranger proved that Pete was right.

The McDonalds made a trip into nearby Polson one day, and their daughter, Lorrie Meeks, recalls clearly what happened. "Dad was getting his hair cut in the barbershop there," she began. "It was one of those old-fashioned establishments where the men would sit and talk for hours just to while away the time. A very elderly man entered the shop, and he and Dad struck up a conversation. This old man knew all about the area near Niarada, and he said, 'You know, around the turn of the century, there used to be an old stagecoach stop there.' Dad told him that he knew about it, adding that the actual site was probably located somewhere on his ranch.

"Dad also mentioned that an old root cellar was still there, and he described just how it was situated. The old man agreed that it must have been the one used by the stagecoach stop to store vegetables. And then he dropped the bombshell.

" 'There was a real nice woman who ran the place,' he said. 'Her name was Hannah Flagg.'

"My dad turned as white as a ghost himself," Lorrie said. "And then he asked the man if he remembered what she looked like. The old fellow thought for a minute, and said, 'I was real young then, but I remember her. She was a very kind woman, and she wore a long skirt with an apron tied around her waist because she was always busy cooking for the customers at the stage stop. She had a couple of little girls, too, but I can't remember their names.'

"My father just couldn't believe what he was hearing," Lorrie said. "As soon as he saw Pete again, Dad confessed to him, 'You know, you weren't dreaming after all. I always thought that the booze was affecting your thought processes, but I guess I was wrong.' And then he told Pete what the old man had said."

Ann McDonald estimates that Pete's encounters with Hannah began over twenty years ago, and she figures that they probably would have continued right up to the present if only the top hadn't come loose from the root cellar about ten years ago. Tom was afraid that his cattle might tumble into the newly exposed opening, so he was forced to fill it in; the McDonalds wonder if somehow Hannah and her daughters got trapped inside during the process. Certainly Pete has never seen them since and, apparently, neither has anyone else.

Skeptics might say that the only spirits Pete encountered were those that came from a bottle. It is true that Pete saw and talked with Hannah primarily when he had been drinking, but even so, how do we explain the fact that the ghost who befriended him so closely fit the description of a real woman named Hannah who had actually worked at the stagecoach stop around the turn of the century? Lorrie Meeks insists that Pete never even knew that such an establishment existed in the area until her father related the elderly man's story to him.

What has become of the ghosts of Hannah and her daughters? To my knowledge, no one has reported any spectral children wandering the area, but Maggie Plummer wonders if a female hitchhiker who vanishes between Niarada and Elmo might be Hannah. Has she been forced from her closed-in root cellar and opted instead for adventure on the road? We'll probably never know for sure, but it's likely that the friendly lady spook will always seek the company of like-minded souls, whether they reside in this world or the next.

Eleven

You'd Better Move On

No matter how dignified and reserved people are when they're alive, when their spirits are released into the Hereafter—watch out! Anyone who has ever listened to a ghost story knows that the average spook is about as well-behaved as the average two-year-old. Ghosts, like kids, do the darnedest things—and they usually do them to us, the living.

Mike Thomas (a pseudonym) discovered this for himself back in 1981, when he moved into his uncle's thirty-year-old house in the Rattlesnake area of Missoula. Mike, who was a part-time deejay at station KLCY, soon made himself at home in what had been his uncle's family room, accessible by stairs that descended from the garage. The biggest problem at first was that the little apartment was often gloomy, with light filtering in only through some small windows high on the basement walls.

This dungeonlike room was decorated with a six-point bull-elk rack hanging on a far wall, and Mike slept on a hide-a-bed under the creature's watchful eyes. For six months the young deejay lived peacefully in his uncle's home, but then something or someone began stirring things up.

A chapter called "Drawer" in D. F. Curran's *True Hauntings in Montana* describes Mike's eerie experiences. One night he awoke and went into the bathroom, where he noticed that four towels from the rack had been neatly folded and placed on the floor of the shower. When Mike mentioned this occurrence to his uncle living upstairs, the older man claimed to know nothing about it.

The next unusual incident took place about a week later, when Mike was again roused from sleep, this time by mysterious footsteps that stopped on the far side of his bed. A light by the stairway provided illumination, and Mike quickly turned over to see who had disturbed him. Startled to find no one there, he sat up and heard the footsteps continue around the foot of his bed and stop beside him before fading away.

Growing more and more uneasy, Mike wondered what would happen next. Two weeks after hearing the footsteps, he again awoke in the middle of the night to find himself staring at a strange light coming from an open drawer of his dresser. Puzzled because he knew he had shut all the drawers before going to sleep, Mike jumped out of bed and turned on his overhead light to take a look.

There, shining its beam out of the fully open dresser drawer, was an old flashlight he had had in the Air Force. The flashlight had not worked for three years, and Mike had never changed the corroded batteries inside. This time, however, the beam seemed to be twice as bright as usual.

Curious about whether the flashlight was hot, Mike tapped it with his hand. It felt cool. He switched the flashlight off and then was unable to turn it on again. Next he checked the batteries and found them corroded and apparently lacking any charge.

Mike told his uncle about this latest experience, and instead of laughing at the spooky tales as he had done before, the old man admitted that the odd phenomena were probably caused by the ghost of his wife, who had died after a long bout with cancer. Mike interpreted the strange events as a sign that he should move out, but his uncle insisted that he was not to go on that account.

The old man went on vacation a few days later, leaving his nephew alone in the house. Not long afterward, Mike shared his weird experiences with the radio audience of his friend and fellow deejay, "Murphy in the Morning." The on-the-air interview ended around 7:00 A.M., and Mike left the station to return home. He was not prepared for what happened next.

The house was securely locked, just as he had left it. He used his keys to get inside, then went down the stairs, around the corner, and into the room where he had lived during the past few months. And there, sitting right in the middle of his bed as if someone had carefully positioned it, was the elk rack.

Mike has never been able to explain how the heavy rack made its way onto his bed. The mounted elk's head had been hung on the wall so that the only way to remove it was to lift and slide it off of the nail, and if the rack had somehow fallen it would not have landed on the bed. There was no indication that anyone had entered the house in Mike's absence, and nothing else had been disturbed.

Finding the elk rack on his bed was proof enough for Mike that someone wanted him to leave. He moved out by Thanksgiving, and when he told his story to D. F. Curran nearly five years later, he was unaware that anyone else had had problems in the house. But now he suspects that his uncle knows more than he lets on.

"My uncle, ninety-one years old, still owns the house and lives there," Mike told me in the fall of 1991. "He says that he has never seen or heard anything strange in the house, but I don't believe him. Two of his kids believe that the ghost is that of his wife. She doesn't seem to bother anyone who comes to spend a night or two, or even more. But when somebody moves in to live there, she gets upset and things start happening."

Mike recalls the experience of one young woman who "house-sat" for his uncle while he traveled for eight months. "She never reported anything strange," Mike said, "but a couple of times she thought she heard something walking downstairs. She said it sounded like a dog clicking its nails on the hardwood floor."

A year or so after Mike left the house, the son of a friend of the family moved into the basement apartment. "He paid my uncle a little money for utilities," Mike explained, "but mostly he was there to mow the lawn, dump the garbage, and do other chores in exchange for room and board while he attended the University of Montana. Nobody had told him about what happened to me, so he didn't have any preconceived ideas about the house.

"I had never met him until one summer afternoon at a family gathering at my uncle's place," Mike continued. "At that time, I had been out of the house for a couple of years, and this guy had been living there for eight to ten months. I asked him how he liked living with my uncle, and he said 'Fine.' From that remark I assumed that nothing unusual had happened to him, and I began telling him about my experiences.

"He stopped me before I'd gotten halfway through, and he was almost in a panic," Mike remembered. "He said he'd never told anyone before because he was sure that no one would believe him, but he was really frightened living there. The spirit kept taking his belongings and hiding them. At first he thought his own forgetfulness was to blame, but he soon learned otherwise.

"The ghost would take the wallet that he left on a table and put it in the bathroom," Mike explained. "It took clothes from his closet, folded them, and put them in the dresser. One day he was late for school and he couldn't find his keys. He had become very careful to notice where he put everything so that he could be sure his imagination wasn't playing tricks on him. He got so frustrated on this particular occasion that he finally yelled, 'Enough is enough—give me my @#!*$!! keys!'

"Immediately after this outburst, he heard a rattling sound in the hallway. He left his bedroom, and there on the floor where he had just walked repeatedly in his search for them were the keys. They were right in the middle of the floor where they could easily have been seen or even stepped on. And my uncle wasn't even in the house when this took place."

As far as Mike knows, this young man is the only one who has actually seen the ghost. "On another day when he was rushing around so as not to be late for school, he passed the bedroom off of the hallway," Mike said, "and out of the corner of his eye he caught a glimpse of an old woman sitting in a chair.

"He stopped and looked directly at her for a few seconds, and he noticed that she was wearing a blue floral print dress," Mike recalled. "He wasn't sure whether he blinked or not, but the woman suddenly disappeared. When he told me that, I took him into the house so he could show me exactly where all of this took place. He had seen pictures of my uncle's wife, but he wasn't positive that she was the woman he saw."

Mike has since lost track of the young man who lived with his uncle, and he no longer remembers his name. But he'll never forget the story he told or the look of terror on his face when he learned that Mike, too, had been tormented by the same ghost.

Twelve
....

Ghosts in Greasepaint

Montana has a far richer theater tradition than most states of a similar size and population because of the great number of citizens who became prosperous from mining and other industries around the turn of the century. Because these wealthy inhabitants valued cultural entertainment, they built theaters to feature the world's leading performers. Sarah Bernhardt, Edwin Booth, and the ballerina Anna Pavlova were just three of the performers who graced Montana stages in the past, and the tradition of quality theater and dance has continued to the present.

Another continuing tradition in the state is that of theater ghosts, reported at Helena's Grand Street, at the Virginia City Opera House, and at both Montana State University and the University of Montana. But several other theaters around the state have also reported their share of psychic phenomena, and their stories are equally intriguing.

English teacher and amateur Butte folklorist Alan Goddard recalls that the Montana Theater, originally called the Old Broadway, was haunted. "All that remains of this fine old Butte theater is a lintel with 'The Montana' inscribed on it," he told me. "Built with Copper King money, it was one of the oldest theaters in the Northwest. Butte citizens wanted their own opera house, and they were proud of the gilt and pink rococo-style structure. The Montana also had the distinction of being the place where Clark Gable made his theater acting debut, as did Vivian Vance, who was Butte's favorite resident actress in the old days of stock companies.

"I never saw the ghost myself, but I heard about it from an old stage-hand and president of the stagehands' union," Alan explained. "An apparition supposedly could be seen in the projection booth and upstairs in the fly gallery, but no one on stage could see it even when it was right there with the performers.

"This ghost was not a particularly harmful one, but it definitely made its presence felt. Once or twice when the actors were rehearsing, someone

......

called out 'Clear the stage—everybody who's not supposed to be in the scene should get off.' At this point the actors were shocked, because as far as they could tell they were the only ones on the stage.

"I don't know who the ghost was supposed to be," Alan continued, "but the stagehand told me that when Anna Pavlova was performing the dying swan in Tchaikovsky's *Swan Lake*, the phantom was so enchanted that it hung around to watch the death scene."

Another haunted playhouse that exists no more was Helena's Old Brewery Theater. "This was the site of a former brewery that was converted into a summer stock operation," explained Steve Wing, current production coordinator for the drama department at the University of Montana. "I worked there the summers of 1969 and 1970, and as soon as I arrived I heard that the building was haunted. I was basically a skeptic, but one night I experienced something that made me wonder.

"It was after rehearsal, and about five of us were sitting around in the kitchen area up on the third floor. Suddenly, the door to the lounge just swung open by itself, and we all felt a chill in the air. At first we thought that a slight breeze must have blown the door open, but then we realized that it was actually a hot, still July evening. We shut the door, and about forty minutes later it opened and then shut itself again.

"We started asking around, and we found out that there had been two deaths in the building. A workman fell to his death during the construction of the brewery, and an actor committed suicide there in the early 1960s. He had warned everyone that he was going to kill himself, but nobody took him seriously until he actually did it.

"Lots of strange phenomena occurred in the Old Brewery Theater," Steve continued, "and people attributed them to the spirits of the men who died there. Some of the stories actually predated the actor's death, having been told when the building was still functioning as a brewery, so at least some of the odd events could probably be blamed on the ghost of the workman."

Yet another haunted theater that exists no more was West Yellowstone's Golden Garter. Debbie and Paul Fleming from Seattle were actors there in 1972, and they had an experience so alarming that they still don't know what to make of it.

"One night after a performance, Paul and I were the only people in the theater, and he was practicing something on a piano up on stage," Debbie recalled. "I was sitting about five rows from the front of the house and just a couple of feet from the center aisle. I was watching Paul when suddenly I felt a hand grab my shoulder as if someone were trying to get my attention. I looked back and to the right and was so startled that I jumped out of my seat.

"Frowning down at me was a man, but I could tell he was not flesh and blood. For one thing, he was standing where no person could have been because the seat was in the way. There were no lights on in the house, but I could see his shape very clearly, and his face looked angry and threatening. He was wearing a white t-shirt and he had a tattoo on the arm he laid on my shoulder. I also remember seeing his beard stubble and hair. I saw him for only a second, though, because as soon as I jumped up he disappeared."

A week or so after Debbie saw the menacing apparition, her husband Paul felt inexplicable cold air in his dressing room and heard mysterious creaking sounds. "That same night, one of the theater people who claimed to be a white witch conducted a seance," Paul remembered. "We all sat in a circle and he conjured up the spirit of the ghost who was haunting the theater. The dead man began speaking through one of the actors, whose voice changed to sound like that of the spirit. We asked the entity why he was there, and he answered that he wanted to possess one of the people in our company. We asked him why, but he refused to tell us. Then we asked him what kind of person he'd been in life and, as I recall, he'd been some kind of laborer. He came across as a wicked person, and, finally, the man conducting the seance cast him out in the name of God."

Some time later, Debbie Fleming asked the leader of the seance if he had seen an apparition while the procedure was taking place. "He began to tell me what the man looked like, and I realized that this was the ghost I'd seen, too," she said. "I wouldn't have been so frightened if the seance leader had seen a different entity. That way, I could more easily ignore what had happened to me."

In contrast to the scary spook of the old Golden Garter is the friendly spirit said to haunt the Missoula Children's Theatre, an enterprise that has gained national recognition for its tours throughout the United States and five foreign countries. Whoopi Goldberg is one well-known star who has appeared in a commercial for the theater, and it would appear that the affable ghost named George is another of the organization's fondest boosters.

At least George isn't shy about making himself noticed. Lori Evans works at the theater, and she has sensed a strange presence and heard unexplained knocking sounds in the old building. "And other people heard a commotion from the shop one day when some boards we had stored against the wall went flying across the room," Lori said. "But the ghost often does helpful things, too. One time, for example, a pianist lost her place in the music book, and some invisible person whispered the correct page number to her just in time."

Another ghost noted for its propensity for helping people is the one at the Fort Peck Summer Theatre. This phantom has been known to stop folks from falling downstairs, an act of kindness that may stem from the way the unfortunate soul lost his own life. The rumors vary, but the gist of them is that someone—a workman during the time of construction, a theater manager, a popcorn salesman, a maintenance man, or a stagehand—fell from a rafter or a ladder to his death. According to most of the accounts, the man was working on the light fixtures in the auditorium at the time of the accident, and his spirit seems eager to prevent any other such mishaps from occurring.

Roger Rock, an actor and former technical director, was one of those who was rescued by the kindly phantom. "I used to check the theater at night just to make sure that the boilers had water and that the furnace was working," he explained. "On one of these occasions, I was walking down a dark staircase when I made a misstep and began to tumble down the stairs. I figured I would be killed, but something arrested my fall so that I stopped moving long enough to recover my balance. I didn't feel as though I had run into a wall or anything, nor did I feel as if anyone were catching me or holding me back. It was a very odd sensation, and I don't know what kept me from pitching down those steps."

The ghost has also saved others from falling. "One guy had his arms so full of bundles of props that he couldn't see where he was going," Paul Fleming remembered. "He tripped and would have fallen all the way to the basement, but an unseen force pushed him back up and held him straight. The bundles fell to the bottom of the stairs, and he just stood there watching them."

A short article written in 1976 by the seasonal director, Kenneth Ott, refers to another man, Gordon Hayes, who was saved from falling down the same stairs. This piece appeared in one of the programs, and it also mentions that Gordon's wife, Peggy, saw the ghost in human form one night in the basement costume shop. "It closed the door and came down the stairs, and then I ran," she is quoted as saying. The article says that the phantom had also unlocked doors and caused things to move suddenly. "Sometimes the ghost talks, and sometimes when the theater is dark and empty, the ghost skips down the aisles. And then some say the ghost shows old movies he loved back in the twenty-four-hour movie theater days," Ott adds.

This is a reference to the early history of the Fort Peck Theatre, erected in 1934 to entertain the more than ten thousand workers and their families who lived in the area during the construction of the Fort Peck Dam. Part of Franklin Roosevelt's New Deal, the construction of the dam continued at all hours of the day and night, and at the end of their shifts, workers were eager to go to the theater to see the latest movies, which were run all day and all night, seven days a week.

"During the wintertime, the theater served another purpose," explained Tom LaBonty, who builds sets and does other behind-the-scenes jobs. "Lots of the workers and their families had poorly built temporary houses, and some even lived in dugouts with no heat. This building was heated, so for the price of a movie the families could go inside and keep warm."

Until 1968, the theater was used primarily as a movie house, but in 1970 the Fort Peck Fine Arts Council was established to ensure that the lovely Swiss chalet–styled building would not be torn down by its owner, the Army Corps of Engineers. The next year, the summer theater program was begun, using professional actors from around the country as well as local people. Accounts of supernatural occurrences have been reported ever since.

"I've worked there for eleven years, and every summer the actors or stagehands talk about something the ghost has done," Tom LaBonty said. "And I've had some strange experiences myself. One night, when Mike Maas and I were working at the theater, the participants in a fishing derby were using the auditorium as a meeting hall. We went backstage to repair a light, and after a while the meeting ended and the people left. We stayed a couple of hours afterward, and we kept hearing somebody walking around in the lobby. At first we thought that someone had returned to the theater after forgetting something, but we heard the sounds several times that night. I went to check the lobby more than once, but nobody was there. I realize that the building is old and makes lots of noises, but we couldn't explain those sounds.

"Actors often say that lights turn themselves on, and once somebody found a record playing, even though no one had been in the building for a long time," Tom continued. "If someone had forgotten to turn off the machine, the needle would have gone to the end of the record and stayed there, but the record was still playing, so the machine had obviously been turned on a short time before."

Paul Fleming has heard mysterious whispering and murmuring voices in the lobby when it was empty, and others have reported hearing music and singing on the stage when no one was there. Mike Maas had one of the strangest experiences of this kind when he and three other people returned to the theater for water when their car broke down after a performance.

"Tom LaBonty was filling up the jug at the sink, and I was standing nearby," he explained. "I saw a shadow go by us, and I heard a man's voice say, 'Oh, puke!' I asked Tom if he had said that, and he said he hadn't. He also told me he hadn't heard anyone speaking. The doors had been locked before we went inside, and we looked all over but could find no one."

This incident occurred in late August 1991; the year before, the technical director heard what sounded like a hammer falling on the stage. "He ran back there to see what had made the noise, but he couldn't find anything," Mike said.

Others have also reported hearing hammering noises from the stage area when it was obviously empty. One of the eeriest occurrences of this type happened to Debbie Fleming when she was the business manager at the Fort Peck Summer Theatre. "I opened the building in the evenings for the performance, and I usually got there early since I had to sell tickets," she explained. "One night as I unlocked the front door, I heard a lot of hammering and the sounds of building from the stage. I figured that Gordie, the set designer, had come in to fix something, so I didn't give the sounds much thought. I kept hearing the hammering and the sounds of somebody whistling, and, after working in my office for a while, I decided to go see how Gordie was doing.

"As I walked into the auditorium, I realized that there were no lights on in the stage area. At first I thought that the hammering and whistling must have been taking place in the construction area under the stage, but if that were the case it was strange that I could hear the sounds so plainly. As I got closer to the stage, I could no longer tell where the whistling was coming from. It suddenly seemed to be all-encompassing yet originating from no one place, and I began to feel uneasy. I felt even more uncomfortable when I realized that the hammering sounds were definitely coming from the unlit stage.

"I walked to an area where I could see if lights were on under the stage, and they were not. I walked all the way to the stage, and the hammering continued. I felt that I was right in the middle of it and, even with no lights turned on, I could see clearly that no one was there. I hurried back to my office and stayed next to the windows so that I could see the comforting sight of people passing by on the street while I did the rest of my work."

As frightening as this experience was, Debbie had another that was even worse. "There are restrooms in the lobby, and I was in one of the stalls," she explained. "The door to the restroom was on the right, the washbasins were on the far left, and the stalls were in between. I heard the door to the room open and shut; someone walked in, went over to the sink, washed her hands, and walked out again. The only problem was that anyone doing these things would have passed right in front of my stall, and I could clearly see through the crack in it that no one was there.

"I was so terrified that I didn't even wash my hands. I just got out of there as fast as I could. I didn't see how anyone could have been playing a trick on me, and when I went to look for the others I found that all of them had been on the stage rehearsing the whole time. All the actors were really freaked out when I told them what had happened."

According to the previously mentioned article by Kenneth Ott, the ghost supposedly "sleeps" in the restrooms in the lobby—although why a ghost would need to sleep at all is never explained. Tom LaBonty offers a more logical reason for the psychic phenomena in this part of the building, claiming that the nearby lobby area used to house a small museum with artifacts discovered during the construction of the dam.

No one has ever offered an explanation for the ghostly blue lights witnessed by several people, including Paul Fleming and Randy and Alicia Pugh. Paul has seen the small lights moving around on the stage, and others have reported them floating in the old projector room or somewhere up in the back balcony.

The back balcony is also where the specter of a man has been seen, according to Roger Rock. "He wears khaki workman's clothes with his sleeves rolled up and the old snap-brim type of hat that was worn during the 1930s," he said. "But as soon as he is sighted, he vanishes in an instant."

Because of all the ghostly goings-on at the Fort Peck Theatre, it might be easy to overlook the presence of something that is even more frightening to lots of people—bats. "We have lots of them, and sometimes they dive-bomb us during performances," Roger Rock said, and laughed. "Once I was playing President Roosevelt in *Annie*, and a bat swooped

The exterior of the Fort Peck Theatre, in which a mischievous but kindly phantom "sleeps" in the lobby restrooms and reportedly saves people from falling. *(Courtesy John G. LaBonty)*

down on the kid who was playing my aid. He let go of the wheelchair, and I started rolling into the audience."

With bats, ghosts, and occasionally even human actors providing such excellent entertainment, Montana's tradition of quality theater, as well as psychic phenomena in its theaters, is likely to continue. One thing, at least, is for certain—in a haunted theater, the most dramatic moments often take place *after* the curtain goes down.

Thirteen

The Selfish Spook of Park Street

Most ghosts don't seem to mind having a few not-yet-deceased folks around—after all, scaring the living daylights out of us is a big part of any spirit's job description. But one ornery apparition in Butte around the turn of the twentieth century was so unaccommodating that it drove away everyone who tried to move in with it. No one who still had a pulse was allowed to stay in the phantom's abode; eventually, the structure itself was torn down. It would appear that this spook was too successful for its own good—and where do displaced specters go?

"Ghost Drives Out Tenants Of A Park Street House" proclaims the headline of the *Butte Inter Mountain* for Tuesday evening, August 20, 1901. The subheading tells us more: "People who have resided in the building . . . tell weird tales of strange doings of the wraith, which has been there for more than ten years." What makes this ghost story unusual, according to the unnamed author of the article, is that "those who have come in contact with his ghostship will readily relate their experiences," even revealing the address where everything had taken place, 509 East Park Street.

The *Butte Inter Mountain* was interested in the story because it was "not the idle tale of gossips, nor the experience of imaginative girls or nervous women, but the coherent accounts of sensible, hard-headed, practical miners, men who are not given to imagining things." If we ignore the sexist assumption that girls and women are overly fanciful or nervous, it nevertheless seems odd that miners, who brought more than their share of superstitions to the United States from practically every country in Europe, should be categorized as so lacking in imagination themselves.

However, one of these men so described was M. J. McFadden, the last tenant to move into the Park Street house at the time of the article's publication. McFadden wanted to stay in the house but was so disturbed by the eerie occurrences there that he went to discuss them with Slemons & Booth, the agents for the property. The agents had heard rumors that the house was haunted, but they considered such stories frivolous and had never taken the trouble to investigate them. After hearing McFadden's account, however, Slemons told the *Inter Mountain* that it was time for the tales to be checked out, and that he, personally, would take the reporter around in his buggy for an introduction to the current owner.

The house at 509 East Park Street is described as "an old one, standing high up from the sidewalk," with "a deep cellar, in which provisions are kept." McFadden was happy to give his account to the reporter, as long as everyone understood that even though he could not explain the strange happenings in the house, he definitely did not believe "in spiritualism or ghosts." McFadden's story follows:

> The night after we moved in here we did not get settled and had to put the children on a mattress on the floor upstairs in one room, while my wife and I slept in another room, which still left a vacant one. I was so tired from work and moving that I went right to sleep. About 2 o'clock I heard the front door, which I had locked myself, open and heavy steps were heard ascending the stairs. I had my six shooter by my bed and I got up and went out to look but could see nothing. I thought it might be the children, hitting the floor with their feet, so I went in and laid [*sic*] on the mattress with them.
>
> Immediately I heard the steps again; they came on up stairs, and went into the vacant room. I listened and heard them moving around. Then they turned and came into my room, right straight up to my bed. I raised up in bed, my gun in hand and demanded: "What do you want?" Of course there was no answer, but the steps immediately receded, passing heavily down stairs, and going out the door was slammed. My wife wakened and asked me who was there. I told her no one, but went down stairs at once and there the door was locked fast. Was I frightened? No. I had been through just about such an experience eighteen years ago and was not afraid.
>
> The next night everything was quiet. Then for several nights there was exactly the same performance. Then in the daytime steps would be heard upstairs, walking around heavily. My wife at first went up to see who it was, of course finding nothing. There is no way to get up stairs only the front stairs up which she had to go. I can't explain it but I shall not move, unless something worse happens.

McFadden concludes by saying that he had asked neighbors as well as former tenants whether anything unusual had happened to them at the house. He reports that "their experience is the same as mine, only with more to it." At this point, McFadden refuses to speak for anyone but himself, insisting that Slemons and the reporter should go to interview a Mrs. Thomas, residing at 51 Broadway Alley.

Mrs. Thomas and her "two pretty young girls" all tell substantially the same story, adding that "Mr. McFadden would see more before he got through" with the house. Pressed for an explanation, Mrs. Thomas continues:

> In addition to the steps and slamming of doors; after we had been there some time we used to hear, at 5 o'clock every morning nearly, a little baby crying in agony. We went to work and looked every inch of that house over, and followed many times the voice to the cellar. There it was always so strong we knew it came from there. I don't believe in spirits but I made up my mind a child had been buried in that cellar. Perhaps a murdered baby. So I had the cellar dug up, the floor, and the sides. But we found nothing. Still the pitiful wailing continued. My little children became so afraid of the steps, when they could see no one and of all the rest of it that I had to move all the beds down stairs and we all slept together down stairs. My older girls and my son, John Kitto, who is also a miner, were not at all afraid until—

At this point, Mrs. Thomas hesitates, "but when pressed to tell all she knew, prefaced it by stating that she herself did not believe in it." Her story continues:

> My son came off shift one night and he, being as usual very tired, went to sleep. The next morning he was as white as a sheet, in fact it was weeks before he got over being pale and haggard. When I asked him what was the matter he told me that at last he had seen the mysterious walker face to face, and that he did not care to repeat the experience. "I went to bed, and as usual went right to sleep," he told me. "All at once, something woke me up. It was not the steps or the crying for I had become so used to them I was never awakened by them. It was something which wakened me out of that heavy sleep with a start. I opened my eyes and there, right by my bed, stood a man. I realized it was not flesh and blood, but the man who was always walking about. He looked right into my eyes and I could not stir. He had on a white shirt and black pants, no coat or vest. I do not know how long he stood there but when he took his eyes off my face it seemed to remove the spell and I sat up and made a grab for him. When I took hold of him,

there was nothing there. I heard the heavy steps go away from the bed and out of the room and down the stairs! I was frightened for a moment for I never saw such a face as that man had—all cut up, horrible to look at."

Mrs. Thomas admits that as she herself has not seen the phantom she cannot be sure of its reality. Her son might have had a nightmare, she explains, but as the writer of the piece points out, "she did not explain why they moved immediately from the place."

No other stories are recounted, although apparently the reporter did talk to a number of people who had lived in the house, "some only long enough to go through one experience, others for several months," but "all told the same story." The writer invites anyone interested in the "chance to lay a real ghost" to try to rid the house at 509 East Park Street of its uncanny inhabitant, and he points out that even those "who do not believe in spiritual apparitions or in ghosts, must believe the testimony of truthful, solid citizens, who would have nothing to gain by telling a story with no foundation."

The writer of the *Inter Mountain* article closes by making the observation that any ghost story becomes more believable when people who don't know one another are able to relate the same tale: "Here are many persons, living at opposite ends of the town, not knowing who has occupied the house since they left, or before them, telling their experiences, and the experience of each one is exactly the same, some being more favored than others in these experiences because of their longer stay in the place."

Since so many people had run-ins with the unfriendly phantom, it's too bad that no one offered even a clue to his identity. The face, "all cut up, horrible to look at," suggests that he was the victim of some type of violence, accidental or otherwise, but after so many years that's the only thing we're ever likely to know about him. And now that the house at 509 East Park Street is gone, it's anybody's guess as to what became of the ghost who refused to share it.

Fourteen

Assorted Haunted Houses of Helena

D uring its heyday as the "Boston of the West," Helena had more millionaires than any other city in the United States. The City of Gold no longer claims this distinction, but it just may hold some kind of record for haunted houses, since so many of the mansions built by wealthy citizens around the turn of the century have now acquired their very own ghosts.

Just ask nineteen-year-old Molly Adams (a pseudonym) on the south side of town. She lives in a century-old house built to be Helena's first and only black Methodist Episcopal Church. "Thank God it isn't haunted — it doesn't even have a graveyard," Molly told me. "But the house across the street is a different story. I've had scary experiences involving that place ever since I can remember."

The small, dark, gingerbread-style structure with cream-colored trim and a turret is about the same age as Molly's house. Two of its oddest features are a cement retaining wall and a yard sunk about six feet below sidewalk level. Molly's first unusual experience with the house took place in that yard.

"I was probably in kindergarten or first grade, and like every kid that age, I liked to go roaring around the neighborhood on my 'hot cycle,'" she explained. "One day I rolled up onto the curb outside the house, and for some reason I can't remember, I just sat there staring at the apple tree. It wasn't a particularly windy day and no one else was in the yard, not even any squirrels. After a few minutes, one of the branches began moving straight downward two or three feet as if someone were pulling it. As the limb neared the ground, an apple popped right off the end of it and the branch swung back up.

"I ran home, yelling for my mother. I told her what had happened, and she tried to reassure me that the wind had caused the branch to move. But I don't understand how the wind could have blown just one limb and none of the others, and I don't see why wind would blow a branch straight downward anyway."

Molly's next unexplainable occurrence took place a few years later, when she was nine. "We lived in the basement of our house for about five years while we were remodeling," she explained. "The first night we got to sleep upstairs was a really big deal. I had my own bedroom, but that night the only furnishings were a shade on the window and a mattress for my bunk bed. I was scared of all the horrible things that I thought were going to get me, and I was also bothered by a streetlight shining in the window and right onto my face.

"I got out of bed to pull the shade down, and I stood looking at the house across the street. I was at the same level as the attic window in the turret, and inside it I saw a perfectly round gold light, about eight inches in diameter. It was a bright, even light, but it didn't seem to illuminate anything. As I watched, it began to swing in a pendulum motion in and out of my range of view. It moved very slowly, coming back into view every ten or fifteen seconds.

"I don't think there were even any people living in the house at the time," Molly continued, "and I have no idea what this thing was. After I'd watched for a minute or two, the light moved close to the window and halted there. I had the strangest feeling that it was a ghost watching me. I pulled the shade down and jumped back into bed."

Apparently, Molly wasn't the only person who was bothered by the house. "There have been lots of renters there—as many as six or seven families in one year was not unusual," she claimed. "Most people didn't stay there long, and two of the families who left admitted that the ghost was the reason for their move. Single people or couples don't seem to have as much trouble there as families with children do, and the phenomena are similar to poltergeist activity in that they get worse when people are having problems."

Molly's most traumatic experience occurred when one of these unhappy families was living in the house. "I was in fifth or sixth grade and I was friends with Chrissy, a girl two or three years younger than I, who lived there," Molly recalled. "One summer day she and I planned to go on a walk with some other neighborhood kids. Chrissy went through the back door to get her shoes, and most of the kids followed her into the living room. I stayed in the kitchen, though, because I'd spotted a cookie jar on the counter.

"To reach it I had to press my chest against the counter and extend my arm full length to pull it forward," Molly continued. "I lifted the lid and looked inside, but there were no cookies. Disappointed, I replaced the lid and slid the jar back until I heard it clunk against the wall. I was just turning to go out when I heard a grating sound. I turned around in time to see the cookie jar scoot across the counter and fly eight feet in the air toward me.

"It landed at my feet, unbroken, and the lid popped off. I screamed and went into shock. I sensed that something was moving around me in a circle, and I kept revolving with it. I was very aware that this thing was taunting me in some way. Then I felt it going out the door of the kitchen."

Molly heard of other weird phenomena that occurred during the time that this family resided in the house. "Doors often slammed for no reason, and the ghost seemed to have a fixation with the bathroom," she said. "One day the father went in there and found the caps off of every single bottle. The contents of some of the containers had been poured into the tub. And when things were missing—shoes, dish towels, or whatever—the family often found them in the bathtub, too."

Over a year ago, the property was finally sold by a woman who had lived in the house for forty years before renting it out. "When she was young, this woman discovered the existence of the ghost, and she apparently made friends with it," Molly said. "She once told my mother that the phantom was that of a fourteen- or fifteen-year-old boy who died in the attic room while his father was building the house. The woman had many experiences with the spirit, and all of them were benevolent and nonthreatening. I remember that when she was packing her boxes to move, somehow they kept getting unpacked. The ghost didn't want his good friend to leave."

Similarly, the phantom apparently felt the need to check out new residents in the house, as it did with two elderly women on their first night in the place. "Their names were something like Eleanor and Joanne, and they had a dog named Daisy," Molly remembered. "Downstairs there are two adjacent bedrooms with a door opening between them. Each woman had her own room, and the dog was lying next to Eleanor's bed.

"Eleanor was just drifting off to sleep when she heard footsteps echoing down the hallway. They went past her bedroom and all the way up the stairs into the attic. Daisy was growling, and her hackles were up. Eleanor's first thought was that there was a burglar in the house, but she decided that it was wiser to stay in bed and to pretend to be asleep than to confront someone who might be dangerous. Minutes passed, and she didn't hear anything else; she finally decided that Joanne must have been the one whose footsteps she heard.

"The first thing next morning, when Eleanor walked into the kitchen, Joanne asked her if she'd gone upstairs the night before. It turned out that both women had heard the same thing, and each assumed that it was the other taking a midnight stroll. After that first night, they never again experienced anything out of the ordinary."

The most recent occurrence of which Molly is aware took place after some very old lilac bushes in front of the house were removed. "In the autumn of 1991, repairmen cut them down to provide access to the foundations of the house," she explained. "The new owner was at work at the time, and he was very unhappy when he found the lilacs gone. A day or so after the bushes were destroyed, some friends dropped me off around two o'clock in the morning. From across the street, I heard sounds of crying coming from the huge pile of branches that hadn't yet been carted away. I was disturbed by the sound, but I couldn't bring myself to walk over there and find out who was sobbing. I had the feeling it was the ghost, crying for the lost lilacs."

Another entity with a proprietary interest in its old stomping grounds is the one haunting the T. C. Power House at 600 Harrison. No one is certain of the identity of the spook at this luxurious west-side mansion, but most people believe it to be a past resident—a former maid, Bishop Gilmore, or Thomas C. Power himself.

The son of Irish immigrants, Power was born in 1839 in Dubuque, Iowa. He first came West in 1860 as part of a survey party for the federal government. In 1865 he settled in Nebraska, moving on to Fort Benton, Montana, two years later. There he opened a general mercantile firm and began freighting operations both overland and down the Missouri River on steamboats. In 1878 he moved to Helena, where he founded or invested in over ninety-five companies during his long and varied career. Power's business interests, to name only a few, included mining, banking, ranching, and lumbering, and he also found time to serve one term in the U.S. Senate.

In 1889, he and his wife, Mary Flanagan Power, built their splendid residence with limestone from one of Power's own quarries. The Powers were fond of living the high life, and they often threw elegant parties for their many friends. The house passed on to their son, Charles Benton Power, who in turn left it to the Catholic Church.

In 1979 and 1980, Pete Ruzevich lived in the Power House as a caretaker for the Catholic archdiocese. "One of the priests told me that my bedroom still had all the original furnishings from Power's time and that

The T. C. Power House, at 600 Harrison, Helena. Music and laughter have been heard coming from an empty top-floor ballroom—are these the ghostly remnants of splendid parties held long ago? *(Courtesy Montana Historical Society, Helena)*

the bed I was sleeping in was the one in which he died," Pete explained. "It was fun to bring dates home to impress them with 'my house,' and to scare them by showing them this bed.

"Once I had a woman over, and I was making up all kinds of stories about how Power's spirit was still in the house. I said, 'One of the things he does is to turn the lights on and off, and he especially likes to put out this oil lantern.' I was telling the woman a fib, of course, but as soon as I said that, the light on the lantern turned bright, then dim, several times over and over as if someone were turning the knob.

"My plan to frighten my date really backfired," Pete admitted. "She thought I was somehow making the lantern act that way, and I was scared to death. It was really kind of funny, but I never figured out how such a thing could happen. The lantern had plenty of oil and I couldn't find any mechanical problems, either."

Two other experiences Pete had while living in the house point not so much to a conscious entity as to psychic impressions recorded on the environment. "Twice as I lay in bed at night, in that stage between sleep and wakefulness, I heard noises from the top-floor ballroom directly above me," he said. "It sounded like a party going on, with people talking and dancing and music playing. That seemed especially odd since the room was being used only for storage.

"The first time I heard the noises I was so frightened that I just lay there trying to convince myself that I was dreaming. Eventually I fell asleep. The second time I heard the sounds, the music was so loud that I forced myself to get out of bed to investigate. I climbed the narrow winding staircase to the ballroom, wondering if I'd lost my mind. I could still hear music and laughter, so I braced myself for a shock and opened the door.

"As soon as I did that, all the sounds stopped," Pete said. "The room was completely dark and empty. I'd never been one to believe in ghosts, but this experience convinced me that something supernatural might very well be going on in the house, that there might be some kind of energy remaining from all those balls the Powers used to host."

After Pete left, Ed Noonan became the resident caretaker for a year, beginning in June 1980. "The diocese hadn't sold the house yet, so there were still a lot of original furnishings on the premises," Ed recalled. "Bishop Gilmore had lived in the house for almost twenty-five years, and in some ways the rooms were more stamped with his personality than with T. C. Power's. One very impressive piece of furniture was the bishop's formal chair that sat in the front foyer.

"One night when I was half asleep, I was startled to hear something down in that area. I was always worried about someone stealing the valuable china and other items on the main floor, so I ran down the stairs to check.

"There's a portrait of Bishop Gilmore in the house, and that night I had the funniest feeling that the man in the portrait was sitting in that formal chair," Ed explained. "I never found a burglar, but the ghost of the bishop ended up in a story I wrote for the *Independent Record.*"

Titled "The Haunted Ballroom," the piece appeared on Friday, October 28, 1988. "The story is fiction," Ed admitted, "although it's based loosely on something that actually happened. On Halloween in 1980, a group of us went up into the ballroom and we turned out the lights and made everything spooky. We'd heard that the ghost of a maid haunts the mansion, and we kept trying to scare each other until one young woman really did get frightened and made us turn on the lights.

"She told us that she had worked in the Power House as a maid when she was younger, when nuns were still living there. The woman said that she'd always had the eerie feeling that people were dancing in the ballroom.

"Some time after Halloween, I saw her again, and she told me that she'd had a strange experience since we last met," Ed continued. "The diocese had sold the house, and it became a day-care center. The woman had gone there one day to pick up her child, and again she had had the odd feeling that people were dancing in the ballroom. I remembered her story through the years, so for the piece in the newspaper I changed the names and embellished the woman's story as my Halloween offering for 1988."

No embellishments are needed to tell the story of another fine Helena mansion, the Kleinschmidt House. Theodore H. Kleinschmidt, who with his wife Mary built the house in 1892, was born in Prussia in 1839. When Theodore was five years old, his mother Louise emigrated with her children to the United States, where she planned to join her husband, who had made the journey earlier. Upon Louise's arrival in the U.S., however, she received the tragic news that her husband had died on the day she and her children first sailed.

The family moved to St. Louis, where Louise eventually remarried. For a time Theodore worked in his stepfather's store, but in 1864 he came to Virginia City with a team of mules and a stock of merchandise. He sold the goods in six months and invested in placer mines, ran a store in German Gulch in Deer Lodge County, and served on the vigilance committee. In 1866, he and partner Samuel Hauser opened the First National Bank of Montana in a grocery store. Theodore Kleinschmidt soon became one of the most active and enterprising businessmen in Helena, with interests in electric lighting, artesian wells, livestock, mining, and other businesses. He was elected mayor three times.

His wife, Mary Margaret Blattner, was born in St. Louis in 1843, after her father, a Swiss instrument maker, emigrated to the United States with his family and all his employees. It was in St. Louis that Mary met Theodore Kleinschmidt, but she married a man with the surname of Westerborg, who was killed in the Civil War. Theodore had always been in love with Mary, so when he learned that she'd been widowed, he headed for St. Louis and convinced her to marry him.

The wedding took place in 1867, on the deck of a river steamer at Fort Benton. Mary and Theodore had four boys and two girls, but one of the girls died in infancy. When the family moved into the red brick Queen Anne–style home in 1892, most of the children were practically grown.

Current owner Janet Sperry, the registrar at the Montana Historical Society, bought the gingerbread-trimmed house in 1972, and caring for it has been her labor of love. "When I bought the property, it was quite

The Kleinschmidt House, at 1823 Highland Avenue, Helena, shortly after its construction in 1892. Current residents believe its ghosts to be Mary Kleinschmidt, who died here in 1904, and her youngest son, Erwin. *(Courtesy Montana Historical Society, Helena)*

run-down," Janet said, "and the real estate agent told me, almost as an after-thought, 'Oh, there's a ghost. She's always upstairs and you can always smell perfume.'

"I've never smelled the perfume, but I've definitely come to believe that a spirit resides here. At first I thought people were saying the place was haunted just because it was an old three-story house that needed a lot of work. But when my two daughters and I moved in, both kids talked about the ghost, so I said, 'If we have one, it's going to be friendly.'

"Before too long my youngest daughter, Elizabeth, started mentioning 'the lady.' For quite some time, I thought she was referring to a figure on the fireplace tile—a reclining dancing girl with a tambourine. But after years of hearing Elizabeth talk about 'the lady,' I began to realize that she was referring to someone else.

"I couldn't help wondering whether her unseen companion had been Mary Kleinschmidt, who died here in 1904 and whose funeral was also held in the house," Janet said.

Elizabeth, now twenty-three, doesn't remember having an invisible friend when she was small, but she does recall several strange incidents that happened just before and during her teenage years. "When I was eleven or twelve, I occasionally heard someone walking up the stairs when I came out of the bathroom at night," she said. "One time the footsteps really scared me. Just as I left the bathroom I heard the unmistakable sound of somebody walking up the uncarpeted wooden stairs. I kept moving until I reached the hallway, where I stopped to listen. Whoever it was took three more steps and halted almost at the top of the stairs. I looked over to where the sound was coming from, but no one was there. I was so spooked that I ran to my room and hopped back into bed."

Elizabeth recalls a night around this same period when her sister Susan and a friend from across the alley were babysitting her. "The older girls were joking and picking on me so much that I went into my bedroom and closed the door," she explained. "I refused to let my sister into the room, and I went to lie on my bed. I was crying hard when suddenly I heard a woman's voice say in a soothing tone, 'Shhh, it's okay.'

"I sat up, and, of course, no one else was in the room. I was so frightened that I went back to be with my sister and her friend. At that point, I didn't care whether they picked on me or not."

On other occasions Elizabeth heard what sounded like footsteps in the ballroom and two people having a conversation in the hallway near the TV room. She also thought she heard them talking when the microwave was on. "Several of my friends refused to stay in the house because of odd sounds or strange feelings," Elizabeth said. "But a braver friend, Terri, spent quite a lot of time there, and she and I had a couple of eerie experiences when we were together. Once, when I was about fourteen, Terri was staying the night and she woke me up, scared to death.

"She told me that she had awakened to see a little blond-haired boy with a hat and knickers standing at the foot of the bed. Her description sounded very much like the youngest Kleinschmidt child, Erwin, who had carved his initials all over the house when he was little. We had a picture of this boy, but Terri had never seen it."

Another time, Elizabeth was in her room getting ready to go somewhere with Terri. "She had been talking to me in my bedroom, but then she left to go sit in another room," Elizabeth recalled. "I was sitting at a vanity table with my back to the door, and I heard her return and stand on the other side of the doorway. She asked me something and I answered. Then she said something I didn't understand about the bathroom and I turned around to ask what she meant. I heard her say, 'Oh, never mind.'

"When I was ready to leave, I walked out into the hallway to ask what she'd been talking about. But Terri wasn't there—she was sitting on the couch in another room, and she claimed she'd been there since she left my bedroom the first time. So I guess I must have been talking to Mary."

On another occasion Elizabeth was trying to make burritos, but every time she returned to the kitchen she found that the oven had been turned off. All present in the house denied having been the culprit, just as they did during the strange episode of the missing jewelry.

When Elizabeth turned sixteen, her mother gave her a pearl and diamond necklace that she had had when she was the same age. "One night I took the necklace off and left it lying on my dresser," Elizabeth said. "The next day when I went to put it on, it was gone. I looked everywhere but didn't find it, and I even wondered if the cat had taken it. My mother and I were both very upset, but there was nothing we could do.

"Almost a year later, my mother was cleaning out the cotton ball jar that sits on the back of the toilet. She pulled the cotton out and there was my necklace in the bottom of the jar. She had cleaned the jar several times after I lost the necklace, and it had not been there. So we decided that Mary must have been to blame."

Mary was also blamed for the disappearance of a stack of college registration papers and other documents that were sitting on Susan's bed. Those have never been found.

A similar event from Susan's college days is what convinced Janet that there really was a ghost in the house. "Susan was attending the University of Oregon in Eugene, and on Christmas break she had brought my present home with her," Janet recalled. "On Christmas Eve, she told me, 'Mom, Mary's taken your present.' She claimed that the present had been in her room, and when she went to wrap it, it was gone. She told me that she had looked everywhere, but somehow it had gotten misplaced. We never did find it in time for Christmas.

"About nine months later, Elizabeth came home from school one afternoon to find a blouse spread out on her bed. She had no idea how it got there and neither did I, but it was the Christmas present Susan had bought for me the year before. I just laughed and said, 'Thank you, Mary.' But I can't help wondering just what use a ghost could have for all our things."

As well as getting to know Mary firsthand at home, Janet has learned a lot about her and the other Kleinschmidts through her job at the Montana Historical Society. "It's such fun to see and handle artifacts that actually belonged to them," Janet said. "And I've also learned a great deal about the family from Mary's grandson, who visits me from time to time."

Janet usually enjoys living in the former home of the Kleinschmidts, but she admits that on one occasion she was frightened. "One winter day a few years ago, I was home alone with two cats," she remembered. "I'd taken the dogs to the kennel because I was going somewhere the next day. At bedtime I went downstairs to put the teakettle on and I wasn't thinking a thing about ghosts. When I headed back upstairs and got to the top of the landing, I walked through the coldest thing I've ever felt in my life. All my hair was standing on end, and I called, 'Mary, is that you?'

"I got no answer, but I was so shaken that I went to sit on the couch with my cats on either side of me to keep me company. I stayed there for quite a while, until I realized that I'd left the kettle on. I went back down the stairs, but this time I didn't run into that cold spot."

Janet felt leery about being alone after this incident, so she called Elizabeth, who was living elsewhere, to come over for a while. "When my mother told me what she had experienced, I remembered the same thing happening to me when I was small," Elizabeth said. "I felt as if something had gone right through me, giving me goose bumps and making my heart pound."

A friend of Elizabeth's once brought her tarot cards to the house, and she told the Sperrys that she had never before gotten such a clear reading. The energy was extremely strong at the top of the stairs, and the reader was sure that it was emanating from a female with an intense attachment to the property.

Because the stairway is one of the most psychically active parts of the house, it's especially fitting that Janet has hung pictures of the Kleinschmidt children along its walls. Both she and Elizabeth believe that this goodwill gesture may have helped to put Mary to rest, because the ghost doesn't seem to make her presence felt as often as before. It's likely that Mary also appreciates the annual visits to her grave on Memorial Day, when Janet and Elizabeth bring her fresh peonies from the garden.

The declining frequency of the phenomena over the years might indicate that Mary is satisfied that someone is taking good care of the home she treasured so much. "Or she might be staying away because she doesn't like our dog Pearl, a huge black Labrador," Janet said.

Now that Mary doesn't come around very often, Janet admits that she wouldn't mind conjuring up another spirit—that of Helena's own Gary Cooper, who was born in one house in the city and lived in two others. "I've been trying to get him to come here for years," she said with a laugh. "When the Marcum family lived in this house, Gary Cooper used to pull taffy right here in the kitchen. I've got two friends who also

Marie Kleinschmidt (Southworth), with brothers Eugene and Erwin. The ghostly shade of a child looking like Erwin has been glimpsed in one of the bedrooms of the Kleinschmidt House. *(Courtesy Montana Historical Society, Helena)*

live in Gary Cooper houses, and they'd like a visit from him, too. Of course, even if we could conjure him up, he wouldn't say anything—he'd just stand there and be masculine."

Another undeniably masculine spirit is that of Judge Theodore Brantly, who apparently haunts what the *Independent Record* referred to as "Helena's Haunted House." In fact, the article by Tom Palmer, published on October 29, 1984, makes clear that the judge was guilty of a charge made against many ambitious men—that he worked so long and so hard that he never found time to enjoy his family.

Ironically, although Judge Brantly spent little time with his wife and children, falsely believing there would be time to do so later, he was fascinated by family members he'd never met. As a boy he was told that his roots extended back to the American Revolution, and he spent a great deal of time and effort through the years verifying this claim.

Born in Tennessee in the 1850s, Brantly came to Montana Territory in 1877. Soon after arriving, he became the first faculty member of the College of Montana in Deer Lodge. He later started a law partnership that eventually failed, and in 1887 Brantly became a justice of Montana's Supreme Court.

As a justice, he began to show his proclivity for long hours and over-work. As Tom Palmer makes clear in the *Independent Record* article, this unusually strong drive was Brantly's dark side, which would "ultimately leave him empty and restless . . . even beyond the grave."

When the judge and his family moved to Helena, they built a three-story house high on a hill at the base of Mount Helena. Originally named Spruce, the street was later renamed Holter. A room on the third floor became Brantly's private study, where he immersed himself in work and in his family lineage.

Eventually he learned from his cousin, Duncan J. Millan, that the family roots did indeed go back to the American Revolution, and that a great-great-grandfather, Neill Smith, had been an officer in the Colonial army. Millan informed Brantly that Smith had been buried on the prop-erty of a man named H. G. Hill. He also mentioned the name of an aunt, Caroline Stevenson.

By what is probably no more than a strange coincidence, the names "Hill" and "Stevenson" would be important later in the history of Judge Brantly's house. For in 1919, the tireless workaholic no longer had the vibrant health or boundless energy he once had, and, as if sensing that the end was near, he sold his home to an Augusta F. Hill for one dollar. Oddly enough, the house was sold twenty-six years later to an Emma Stevenson.

Judge Brantly died in 1922, but not before admitting to his friends that he'd spent far too much time building his career and far too little time being with his loved ones.

The house on the hill was sold again in 1963, and for the first time in the mansion's history, the owners had no connection to the Brantly family, although like the Brantlys, the family, called the Dixons (a pseudo-nym), had a daughter and two sons. The Dixons began removing walls to remodel the interior in the late 1960s, and according to the *Independent Record* article, that's when the weird phenomena began to occur.

"It was like we disturbed something," Mrs. Dixon is quoted as saying, and she added that the ghostly goings-on were so persistent that one of the sons actually began to hate the house. He reportedly felt as if someone were trying to "get close to him" while he was in what used to be Judge Brantly's study. The television in this room would often turn itself on after being shut off, and when Mrs. Dixon was alone in the house she frequently heard footsteps slowly ascending the steps to the third floor. She heard them all day long, and they sounded so forlorn and sullen that they made her nervous.

The Dixons weren't sure what the ghost's intentions were, but the author of the article suggests that the judge's spirit simply wanted to spend time with the children, because he'd missed out on the growing up of his own daughter and two sons. Whatever the reasons for the phenomena experienced by the Dixons, strange things continued to happen to later occupants, and they were not always interpreted as benevolent.

The house was eventually converted into apartments, and one absentee owner hired a caretaker to live in one of them. The phantom became increasingly aggressive, so much so that the caretaker was forced to move out. According to the *Independent Record* article, he often heard the forlorn footsteps treading the stairs, and the vacuum cleaner sometimes turned itself on.

But the most alarming occurrence involved a large rhododendron plant that the Dixons had left behind in the judge's old study. The caretaker is quoted as saying that the plant "lifted off the floor and shook itself and then [it] just fell over dead."

The family of Kathleen Dombvski moved into one of the apartments in the house in 1977, and they experienced something odd on their very first night. "We had the kids' beds set up for them, but my husband and I slept huddled on the couch together," she told me. "In the middle of the night, I woke up and heard something rolling around on the floor. My husband was also awake, and his first thought was that our Irish setter was chasing something. I pointed out that the dog was right beside us, lying on the floor.

"I got up to see what was happening, and I saw a piece of dry dog food rolling around by itself. It was the craziest thing, because I couldn't understand what was making it do that. I picked it up and threw it away, and we had no more trouble that night."

Two days later the second mysterious event occurred, and it was uncannily similar to the rhododendron episode described in the *Independent Record* article. "We had about eighty plants in the dining room,"

Kathleen said, "and one of them, a spider plant with lots of 'babies' trailing from it, suddenly flew straight up in the air, came back down, and wobbled for a second or two. I stared at it, wondering what in the world had caused it to shoot up like that."

While Kathleen's family was living in the house, two other incidents occurred that were also reminiscent of those reported in the newspaper story. The vacuum cleaner once switched itself on, just as the caretaker's had done. "My husband and I were standing in the living room when the sweeper started up in the kitchen," Kathleen recalled. "No one was even close to it when that happened."

The other similarity involved the disappearance of candy. The Dixons reported that sweets vanished from trays, and Kathleen recalled the experience of a woman who lived in the basement. "This lady loved M&M's, and she always kept a clear glass bowl filled with them," Kathleen said. "One night after she had gone to bed she was awakened by the sound of someone scraping the sides of the candy dish, then letting the M&M's fall back in.

"She got up and noticed that half the M&M's were gone. She thought that somebody must have come into the house, so she turned on the lights and checked the doors, but no one was there. The next night the same thing happened, and she decided that a band of M&M-loving mice might be to blame. To keep them from getting her goodies, she cut a piece of paper to fit tightly over the top of the bowl, just below the rim.

"A couple of nights later, she heard the same sound of candy rattling around in the bowl," Kathleen continued. "She listened for a while, then got up to see what had happened. The paper was still in place, but every one of the M&M's was gone. The lady moved out of the house shortly afterward."

Kathleen and her family didn't take long to become disenchanted with the house, either. The kids and the dog hated going into the attic, even though it had been made into a play area. And they were all tired of the loud banging noises from the basement, which had started just a night or two after the family moved in. "We were sleeping, when suddenly we heard what sounded like someone trying to move the washer and dryer," Kathleen explained. "We called our neighbor who lived downstairs, and he told us he'd assumed that we were the ones making the racket. Afraid that we were being robbed, we went to investigate. We didn't find anyone in the basement, and the noises stopped, only to start up again later, several nights in a row. During the six months we lived in the house, we heard the same banging noises on an average of twice a week."

Kathleen also recalls seeing a tiny bright light, almost like a firefly, zooming around the corner of the living room and going past her. By the time she turned around to see where it went, it had disappeared. This occurrence was repeated on several nights when she went to check on her two-year-old son, Nate.

Kathleen's husband had lived in the house for six months before his family joined him, and he had come to believe that several unseen entities were responsible for the spooky events. His own father in Connecticut lived in a haunted house, and the older man warned his son that if there was even an inkling of danger the family should get out of the place at once.

"I never felt that anything bad would happen, but once when Nate fell on the spiral staircase on the way to the attic, he hurt himself quite badly," Kathleen said. "I couldn't help wondering if that was the start of a series of harmful occurrences.

"About a week after Nate got hurt, my daughter Holly and I were sweeping when the vacuum cleaner belt broke. We were listening to the song, 'Marie, the Dawn is Breaking,' while I took the machine apart to put a new belt on it. Suddenly, from the attic, we heard shuffling sounds as if people were waltzing.

"We knew that no one should have been up there, and when Holly asked what was going on, I admitted that I didn't know," Kathleen said. "When the song ended, so did the shuffling. I decided to confront whatever spirits were in the house, so I told them that we'd had no other choice of a place to live, and that we were trying to make the best of the situation until we could find a better house. The ghosts would just have to put up with us until then.

"After my outburst, all the strange phenomena stopped. But a while later, the woman who owned the house decided that she would make more money by excluding children. We obliged her by agreeing to move out.

"The very day she asked us to leave, weird things started happening again," Kathleen recalled. "The banging noises from the basement resumed, lights started whizzing past me in the living room once more, and Nate began having nightmares that someone was in his closet.

"Two weeks later, we left; I don't know who lives there now or if anyone after us has had any problems in the house."

Kathleen does have a theory about the cause of the haunting, however. She believes that whoever the entity may have been, he or she was registering a protest about the way the once-lovely mansion was remodeled. "It looked really tacky when we lived in it—the ghost probably couldn't stand that red velvety stuff on the wallpaper."

No one fully understands why phantoms do what they do, but for some reason they do an awful lot of it in Montana's capital city.

Fifteen

Montana Ghost Lights

Since the earliest times, whenever people have come together to talk about the strange universe they inhabit, they have told one another stories of mysterious orbs of light, large and small, that appear to move all by themselves through the nocturnal landscape, usually just a few feet off of the ground. Called everything from "ghost lights" to "witches' lanterns" to "will-o'-the-wisps," these glowing globes have been reported, photographed, and even videotaped all over the world and are almost certainly a natural phenomenon, although to this day no one knows what they are.

Ghost lights seem to be reported more often in rural than in urban areas, perhaps for the simple reason that they show up better on dark country roads and fields than on well-lit city streets. They range in size from a few inches to a few feet across, and they appear to be as close as a few yards or as far as a mile or two away from their observers.

This mystifying phenomenon was reported in the Montana press as early as March 23, 1881, when Helena's *Daily Herald* ran a story titled "Ghostly Visitations!" According to the article, some eerie lights had been "seen moving about, of their own accord apparently, over the farm and around the house and outbuildings of the late Charles Tacke, who was murdered last fall by Peter Pelkey." Pelkey had been hanged, but the mysterious lights suggested to certain observers that the spirits of the two dead men were still not at rest.

The earliest reports of sightings came from farmers and ranchers whose property adjoined the Tacke farm, and they insisted that they had seen the lights "almost ever since" the murder. "For a while no attention was given them," the unidentified writer of the article explains, "but so often have people who were passing the Tacke ranch in the night seen these lights and told about them on their arrival here, that night before last a party of our citizens, who have the organ of inquisitiveness developed to a little more than the ordinary, concluded to ride down to the ranch and witness for themselves the phenomena, if such there were."

These curiosity-seekers began by interviewing everyone they could find who had seen the lights. One informant was a "stolid German farmer" who "told his story with all gravity, and whose word [the investigators] would not think of doubting." This forthright farmer declared that he had seen the lights just as snow began to fall, and they "looked like the light thrown from a red glass lantern at first, but have been growing paler and lighter in color ever since." He had seen from one to four of them in one evening, moving about, "some going up as high as twenty feet and moving around in different directions, and sometimes, apparently, settling on the corners of the fence." The lights would begin moving again around the house, barn, and corrals, before "finally sinking down and disappearing in an instant, leaving darkness behind."

Another farmer claimed that he first saw the lights when the days began growing shorter in early autumn. He described the objects as "clear, bright lights, moving slowly about the open fields, and sometimes rising to a considerable height in the air, going over and around the house and barn, and visiting the pig pens, chicken houses, corral and either suddenly disappearing or rising up and sailing slowly across the valley until they were lost to view."

The farmer's interrogators add a wry and cautionary observation at this point: "We should believe this man [more] if we did not know he takes a good deal too much stimulus sometimes to be a good judge of such wonderful sights as he describes, and think his imagination plays him tricks."

In contrast to the farmer, the investigators are described as "sober-minded, reliable men," but they, too, witnessed the ghost lights. Two of them said that as they were traveling the road alongside the farm (presumably Tacke's), suddenly they saw "a large, bright light moving over the open field, somewhere from ten to forty feet above the ground." The orb was "apparently from four to six inches in diameter and from eighteen to twenty-four inches high, the body of the light being of an orange color, occasionally flashing off rays of a greenish or sometimes of a bluish tintage, to a distance of forty or fifty feet." This object, which sounds like a tiny UFO to modern readers, moved slowly up, down, and over the fields before gradually sinking down and vanishing. The men also saw two other moving lights "which looked like a lamp light surrounded by a porcelain globe, the body of the light not being visible, but white, mild and distinct."

The *Daily Herald* article goes on to state that while no rational explanation for the lights had been found, some observers believed them to signal the end of the world, others thought they were electric lights that had somehow escaped from Edison's laboratories, and still others believed that they were sent from "h--l" by the murderer to find the place where the murdered man had buried his money.

More than one hundred years later, on December 13, 1987, the *Lewistown News-Argus* published a piece by Gene Meier about ghost lights that had been appearing for generations farther to the east in Fergus County. Portions of the article, titled "Grass Range light remains a mystery," are excerpted as follows:

> One of my favorite stories was one my father would tell, generally after dark, while riding in the car on some lonely road.
>
> The story was of a light seen on their prairie homestead which was located approximately ten miles south of Grass Range, Montana. Of course, it was always seen after dark and usually from about 9:00 in the evening till almost midnight. It was like someone walking along swinging a lantern.
>
> The story was told as gospel and there were many witnesses who had collaborated the story. Among those names still around the country are the Ahlgrens, the Schaffs, and the Moultans. My grandfather was reportedly the first person to see it. His first thought was that it was the neighborhood bootlegger John Smith, out on a delivery.
>
> In the weeks that followed the first sighting, it was clear that he was not the culprit. Weather didn't seem to make any difference as to the frequency of the sightings, although most were in the late summer and early fall. It traveled a ten square mile area passing by many homesteads.
>
> During this time, the land grant era, there was a homestead every one hundred and sixty acres. After a period of time, it became well known and occasionally a scared neighbor would take a pot shot at the light. When this happened the light would disappear only to reappear further down the trail.
>
> No one ever found any tracks where the light had been and the closest anyone could ever get before it would go out was about one half mile. My grandparents moved to the homestead in 1907 and stayed for 27 years. When they left the place during the depression, the light was still active.
>
> To this day no one has ever found out what the light was. But there is one more chapter to add to this story. A year or two ago I met the person who now farms the old homestead. Of course, I had

to tell him about the light and its mystique. His eyes grew wide and his face turned white as I told him the story of the light!

When I had finished, he then related his own story of a few weeks earlier. While farming late at night he had seen a light, like someone walking along swinging a lantern! He had told no one of this sighting because of fear of ridicule. I am sure he told the truth. I could see in his eyes the wonder of it all.

When I contacted Gene Meier, he told me that before meeting this man he had always dismissed his own father's tales of the lights as folklore, but he now believes the ghost lights to be a natural, although unexplained, phenomenon. "After all, for centuries nobody knew what the Northern Lights were until scientists began studying them," he pointed out. "Maybe there's a rational explanation for ghost lights, too, having something to do with gases or magnetic fields."

Gene's aunt, Marguerite Maddox, still remembers being frightened by the eerie lights when she was eight or ten years old. "We lived about eighteen to twenty miles south of Grass Range, and my most vivid memory is of one night when we were riding home in the spring wagon with the horses," she recalled. "We lived up on a bench, a high, flat place. And over on the rims about three-quarters of a mile away we could see this light. It seemed to be following the rim, and it swung back and forth looking just like someone walking with an old-fashioned lantern. And, of course, in those days we didn't have electric lights like we do now, so seeing something like that was unusual.

"My dad did a lot of trapping, and often he'd come home at night and say that he had seen the light," she continued. "It never bothered him, but it really spooked me. Some people tried to laugh off the stories of people who had seen it, but then they would see it themselves and it didn't seem so funny anymore. One man who was out herding sheep actually shot at it, but that didn't do any good. And some people would try to get close to it, but they never could because it would just disappear."

A few miles away, in the northern part of Fergus County, George D. Kurns saw ghost lights many times when he was a boy. His parents homesteaded there in 1916, and the mysterious spectacle provided entertainment for his whole family.

"We would look toward the foot of the mountains late in the evening, and we could see a round ball of light floating there," he said. "It would travel for miles, going back and forth down the canyons and hills, and at times it would disappear only to reappear somewhere else. That would happen on clear nights. We sat and watched it for many hours, and I suppose many other homesteaders did, too. It was like a pastime to see it and then talk about it among ourselves. Most people said it was a will-o'-the-wisp."

According to Nancy Arrowsmith's *A Field Guide to the Little People* (New York: Hill and Wang, 1977), will-o'-the-wisps are phosphorescent flames or lights seen in swamps and other deserted places; folk belief for centuries has defined them as lanterns carried by elves who were at one time human beings. "As such," Arrowsmith points out, "they come closer to being 'ghosts' than any other elves. They still remember their lives on Earth, and have not been completely welcomed into the elfin world. . . . On the whole, their relationship with men is good, for they haven't forgotten the ways of their old world and still have compassion for its inhabitants."

Arrowsmith goes on to show that will-o'-the-wisps take different forms in each European country, and that there is even a special sea variety known as "St. Elmo's Fire," believed to be the souls of the drowned. Arrowsmith also notes that will-o'-the-wisps are most apparent in late summer, autumn, and winter, and that they prefer to frequent damp places. If that is true, and the Montana ghost lights are indeed will-o'-the-wisps, they obviously must have adapted themselves to a much drier climate than the one they enjoyed in the old countries.

George Kurns recalled that the "will-o'-the-wisp" he saw often appeared at the site of a deserted gold-mining town named Maiden, and that the presence of the strange light was an indication that something was wrong. "Because many of the dead there had never been buried properly, maybe their souls were not really satisfied," he explained.

Whatever their cause, will-o'-the-wisps were so well known in the state that reference is made to them in Elsie Townsend's novel, *Always the Frontier* (Herald Publishing, 1972), set in Culbertson, Montana:

> Slowly they walked back through the darkening evening. Reaching the kitchen door, Sam turned and looked to the north past the alkali flat, to the low rise a mile away.
>
> He pointed. "Look, Florence—will-o'-the-wisps!"
>
> She turned to look that way. Little splotches of light seemed to be flickering back and forth.
>
> "Looks almost like a man carrying a lighted lantern walking toward the hill," she said. "It's no wonder people used to call them witches' lanterns."

Are these "little splotches of light" the same thing as the mysterious (and usually larger) ghost lights? Or are they separate but similar phenomena, both with unknown causes?

Jerome F. Kolar, an eighty-year resident of central Montana, first heard about so-called "witches' lights" from a hired man. A few years later, in the early 1930s, he actually got a look at them himself.

"My brother and I were moving a band of sheep to summer pasture," he recalled. "We bedded them down for the night at a site east of Danvers, a small town about fifty miles northwest of Lewistown. I noticed the lights that flickered like lanterns against a small incline to the north of us. Because I had never given much credence to the supernatural, I observed the lights for quite some time. The movement resembled that of a honey bee flitting from flower to flower. There were two of these lanterns relatively close to one another. Though they gave the illusion of being far away, I knew the distance could be only a hundred yards or so judging from the distance to the incline.

"For a time the 'lanterns' disappeared, only to appear again farther down the stream. Then I realized that these were fireflies flitting from plant to plant and giving the effect of someone carrying a lantern."

Although it's likely that people besides Jerome Kolar have occasionally mistaken fireflies (or even the rare phenomenon of ball lightning) for something supernatural, it doesn't seem that they could all have been fooled in this way. In fact, in most accounts of ghost lights from around the world, the objects are usually described as round like a ball, and they are nearly all at least a few inches in diameter. The lights also do not exhibit the rapid flickering of fireflies. Many observers have likened them to automobile headlights or flashlight beams, and neither of these resembles the tiny illumination of a firefly.

So what are ghost lights? Will scientists ever learn their cause? Current theories are that they may be formed in some way by escaping natural gas or by electromagnetic fields; one of the most intriguing suppositions comes from a New Jersey research group called Vestigia, described in Loren Coleman's *Curious Encounters* (Boston: Faber and Faber, 1983). After investigating a ghost light in that state, Dr. C. Louis Wiedemann explained that the light would "bob and sway from side to side in the manner of a swinging lantern, and when approached, it vanishes, sometimes reappearing at a distant site." Because this particular light, like many others around the world, always appeared on or near railroad tracks, the researchers suggested that these lights are produced when certain minerals (such as quartz) are squeezed during earth movements and small earthquakes. The accumulation and subsequent discharge of the resulting electrical buildup through the metal railroad tracks could then conceivably produce the phenomenon of ghost lights (*Curious Encounters,* 83–84).

Apparently, none of the mysterious glowing orbs described in this chapter appeared near railroad tracks, but as Loren Coleman observes in a companion book, *Mysterious America* (Boston: Faber and Faber, 1985), the growing body of scholarship on the subject has also shown "that phenomenon's unique attraction to streams, groves of trees, roads, certain fields, [and] mountains." And, to judge from the accounts given here, the strange balls of light must also be drawn to houses as well as to farm and ranch buildings.

It may be a long time before we know what ghost lights really are, and until then, Montanans might do well to turn off their televisions, sit back, and enjoy a quiet night in the country, on the lookout for one of the earth's most mysterious wonders.

Sixteen

The Lonely Lady and Other Ghosts
of Chico Hot Springs

T he Chico Hot Springs Lodge and Ranch in Montana's aptly named
Paradise Valley is famous for its steaming thermal pools and its
superb gourmet cuisine; but in recent years, it has become almost
as well known for its psychic phenomena.

It isn't surprising that Chico has such star-quality spooks, not when
you consider that the combination restaurant, hotel, and resort is also
a favorite "haunt" of celebrities such as Peter Fonda, Jeff Bridges, and
Dennis Quaid. In the old days, Chico even hosted famed cowboy artist
Charles Russell, who traded drawings on the back of stationery for drinks,
and President Theodore Roosevelt, who stayed there the night before
he visited Yellowstone National Park, thirty miles to the south.

Originally named the Chico Warm Springs Hotel, the establishment
opened to the public on June 20, 1900. Owners Bill and Percie Matheson
Knowles enjoyed the resort as much as any of their guests, although Percie
did have strong qualms about drinking. Over her objections, Bill constructed a saloon and dance hall on the property, and the resort became
even more successful, promoting itself as a place to cure "rheumatism,
stomach and kidney troubles, and all skin and blood diseases."

Perhaps Bill Knowles should have spent more time in the hot pools and
less in the saloon, because on April 22, 1910, he died of cirrhosis of the
liver. He was buried a few days later at nearby Chico Cemetery, leaving
Percie and the couple's twelve-year-old son, Radbourne, to run the business.

Percie's dream was to turn the retreat into a real health-care center,
and her first action was to close the saloon she detested. In 1912, she
persuaded Dr. George A. Townsend to make the hotel his headquarters,
and he was so successful in treating patients that Chico's fame spread
quickly to surrounding states. Over the next five years the pools were
enlarged, and a hospital wing was added.

Dr. Townsend stayed at Chico Hot Springs for thirteen years, but

Percie Knowles in 1915, standing next to a giant sunflower in her garden at Chico Hot Springs. She is believed to be only one of the spooks still haunting the popular resort. *(Courtesy Doris Whithorn)*

finally the hard work became too much for him. He retired in 1925, and even though other doctors came to take his place, the resort would never again enjoy a fine reputation as a hospital.

Radbourne Knowles moved away to get married, and Chico attracted fewer patients every year. As Percie's beloved resort began to decline, so did she. Her mind as well as her body gave way to the pressures of running a failing business, and for a long time she was confined to her room in the hotel. In 1936 she was admitted to the state hospital in Warmsprings, where she died four and a half years later.

After Radbourne's death in 1943, Chico Hot Springs went through a series of owners who couldn't decide whether to make it a health resort, a vacation getaway, or a combination of both. In 1973, Mike and Eve Art bought the property, and three years later they moved from Cleveland, Ohio, to live on it. Since then they've made many improvements, so that once again Bill and Percie's resort is thriving.

And so is the ghostly activity at the old lodge. Could the Arts' refurbishment of Chico have caused the burst of psychic phenomena reported by guests and employees alike? This might be possible, except that former owner John Sterhan recalls that during his tenure, from 1967 to 1972, the staff also reported strange events. The most common belief among those who have had eerie encounters at Chico is that the Knowleses, especially Percie, have never left.

Earl Murray wrote about the otherworldly occupants of the resort in his *Ghosts of the Old West* (Chicago: Contemporary Books, 1988). In "The Hot Springs Phantom," he describes the weird experience of two security officers, Tim Barnes and Ron Woolery, around 2:20 A.M. one Sunday in May 1986. The two guards had waited for all the customers and employees of the Chico Saloon to leave, then they locked the doors and returned to the hotel via the board walkway. At this time, Tim had been working for the resort for eight years, and he'd never believed his co-workers' spooky stories. Just as he opened the door leading into the lobby, he saw something and suddenly froze.

"Look," Tim said, and pointed across the room in the direction of an old piano.

The two security officers stared in amazement at the sight before them. A white filmy figure hovered just above the floor near the piano, and the smoky features of a face stared back at them. Only the head and upper body were distinct; the rest of the apparition was a formless mass trailing away to nothing.

"It was an eerie feeling, the kind that makes the hair stand up on the back of your neck," Tim said, when I interviewed him in October 1991. "I wasn't afraid of it, but I realized that we were definitely looking at something supernatural. We kept staring at the ghost, and I finally got the idea to take a picture of it with a Polaroid camera in the office."

To get to the office required courage, because it meant walking close to the figure. Tim steeled himself and hurried around the phantom and through the door. He found the camera, but because it didn't belong to him and because he was nervous, he couldn't figure out how to attach the flash bar.

"I decided to take the picture without the flash, and the results weren't very good," he said. "There's one tiny white unidentifiable spot in the middle of the photograph. Whatever we saw was definitely in the basic form of a person, but we couldn't tell what sex it was. It must have hovered by the piano for a good two minutes, but after I took the picture the hazy form just dispersed like smoke."

Tim is now the general manager of Chico Hot Springs, and he's joined the ranks of those who are certain that the old hotel is haunted. His mother, Edie Mundell, is another person who knows from firsthand experience that the phantom is real. She worked as a night auditor there for three years and had just quit her job when I talked to her, also in October 1991. Edie's encounter was very similar to that of her son.

"I've been interested in metaphysical subjects for a long time, so I thought I'd be well prepared if I ever saw the ghost," she explained. "On the morning when I finally did, everything had been very quiet. I needed to get a printout on the credit card machine, and I walked into the dining room to pick it up. At the same time, the security guard who had just finished his rounds was coming through the front door along with some people working the breakfast shift. I heard them all talking together.

"The dining room was dark because I hadn't turned the lights on," Edie continued, "and for some reason, I suddenly had an impulse to look behind me, through the back of the dining room and into the small lounge. And there, standing at the door to the lounge, was an apparition.

"It was cloudy and all white, just like ghosts are often portrayed in the movies. It was smoky and hazy, but it was shaped like a person. I think it was a woman, but I'm not sure. Looking at it gave me the weirdest feeling, and even though I thought I would be well prepared for such an encounter, I wasn't. I think I startled that ghost nearly as much as it startled me – I could sense fear coming from both of us. I don't think the spirit noticed me until I began walking quickly away from it. I got out of there before it had time to disappear."

Around the time of my interview with Edie Mundell, bartender Terrie Angell encountered the same apparition in another part of the darkened dining room at about three o'clock one morning. "Even now I can't tell you whether or not I believe in ghosts," she told me, "but I could definitely feel her presence as soon as I walked through the door. And there she was, sitting in a chair on the left-hand side of the room. Because it was dark, I can't describe what she looked like except to say that the image seemed more hazy than solid. I ran out of that dining room as fast as I could; even talking about it now gives me goose bumps."

Fellow employee Lindy Moore was equally terrified by her encounter with the filmy phantom in the winter of 1989. "I had gone up to the second floor to put a blanket in a room, and all of a sudden I became aware that someone else was there," she said. "I turned around and saw the apparition very clearly. I'm sure it was Percie. She was wearing a dress and she appeared to be floating. The figure was cloudy and misty, but I could definitely see her features. She had a fairly blank expression on her face, but I'm sure she could see me.

"I'd never actually seen a ghost before, and it scared the heck out of me," Lindy admitted. "I stood there for probably twenty seconds, and part of me really wanted to stay to find out what would happen next. But when the form started to move toward me, I changed my mind in a hurry and got out of there. Thinking back over the experience now, I believe something very interesting would have happened if I had stayed in the room, but I was just too scared. And I've never seen her since."

Former security guard Larry Bohne has probably gotten a closer look at Chico's lady spook than has anyone else. Larry hastens to explain that he is by nature a highly logical and analytical person, having worked as an air traffic controller for the U.S. Air Force, and as a soils and concrete lab inspector for the U.S. Army Corps of Engineers. His other work, as an ambulance technician and a volunteer firefighter, also required equal measures of cool observation and common sense. Larry had been employed at Chico Hot Springs for about fifteen months when he had one of the eeriest encounters ever reported there.

"It was the third week of January 1990, and I was used to being alone in the old hotel," he said. "During the winter months it usually has only a few guests at any one time, and on this night they were in rooms on the main floor just off the lobby. Besides them and me, the only other person in the hotel was the night auditor in the main office.

"Even though no one was staying on the second and third floors, it was still my job to make routine fire checks in these areas," Larry said. "One one of my rounds, at about 2:30 A.M., I was walking along the second floor hallway, and as I passed the stairwell leading to the third floor I could sense that someone was at the head of the stairs. I stepped back a few paces to the bottom of the stairwell and looked up to see a matronly lady standing at the top landing looking down at me.

"That seemed unusual because I was sure there were no registered guests above the first floor," Larry explained. "The lady appeared to be about five feet four to five feet six inches tall and approximately forty-five to fifty years old. Her face, though clearly defined, seemed pale and without expression. It was obvious that she was looking at me, but she didn't acknowledge my presence in any way. She wore a full-length pale blue dress with a high collar and long sleeves and the material was printed with what looked like tiny white flowers. Her graying hair was in a tight bun, and her hands were clasped in front of her.

"Thinking that she was a guest who had gotten lost, I asked if I could help her. When I spoke, she silently turned away and moved into the darkness of the third floor hallway behind her. I say 'moved,' because she didn't seem to be walking—she just drifted away without any movement of her upper torso. I couldn't even detect any leg movement under the long dress.

"I went up to the main hallway of the third floor, but I could see nothing," Larry said. "Everything was dark except for some soft light from the courtyard below that filtered into the window at the end of the hall. The lady I had seen so clearly just seconds before had vanished.

"All the rooms on that floor are kept locked, so I guessed that the only place she could have gone would have been into one of the bathrooms, which are not locked. As I walked down the hall, I detected a sweet fragrance in the vicinity of rooms 346 through 350. I checked the bathrooms, but they were empty and dark. I retraced my steps down the hallway and again smelled the sweet scent in the same area as before. It reminded me of jasmine or lilac, and it was strongest near room 349.

"I used my security passkey to unlock the door. The room was silent and dark, and I shone my flashlight inside. Then I noticed that the rocking chair in the corner by the window was gently moving back and forth. I quickly flipped the light switch on, and I saw the chair stop rocking instantly, as if someone invisible had been sitting in it and made it stop. I checked the window and noted that it was tightly shut. But even if it had been open, the night was extremely calm, without any wind to make the chair rock. And if the movement had been caused by wind, the chair would not have stopped rocking so suddenly. I also realized that the sweet fragrance that had been so strong before had now completely faded away.

"The entire episode lasted about five or six minutes," Larry said, "and afterward I was eager to return to the reality of the main office and the reassuring company of Edie Mundell, the night auditor. I was so unnerved that it took me several cups of coffee to muster up the nerve to tell her what had happened; when I did, she smiled and said, 'Welcome to the Percie Club.'

"Edie also told me that room 349 was the one in which Percie Knowles had lived during her last days at Chico," Larry explained. "She had become quite senile and spent nearly all her waking hours in a rocking chair, staring out the window at Emigrant Peak behind the hotel."

Security guard Charlie Wells had an experience similar to Larry's when he worked part-time at Chico in 1989 and 1990. But while Larry initially believed that the woman he saw was flesh and blood, Charlie was made immediately aware that the lady ascending the stairs from the second to the third floor was not of this world.

"I came up out of the lobby on one of my rounds, and all I saw at first was a kind of mist," Charlie explained. "I could see features, but it seemed as if I were seeing her through a smoke-filled room. I saw her arms, but no hands and no legs, and I could just make out a face. She appeared to be floating rather than walking up the stairs, and she was wearing a long, flowing white dress. In fact, it looked a lot like the one that Percie Knowles is wearing in a picture hanging in the lobby."

Charlie often had the disquieting experience of finding the door to Room 349 unlocked and open. "This was during the wintertime when business was slow," he said. "I knew the room hadn't been rented out, so I'd lock it up; but the door would be open again when I made my next round. I was the only one there before the auditor arrived, and I was the only one with the keys. The other keys were all locked away.

"Another time, I was locking the outside door to the saloon when I noticed a light on in the lounge," he continued. "A man and a woman were sitting at a table near the window in the dining room off to the right. I couldn't make out many details, but I did see that the woman was wearing a long white dress. I knew that the cooks, the waitresses, and the dishwashers had all left after dinner, and I thought that maybe the owner's daughter, Andy Art, had come back with her boyfriend to have a drink.

"I went on into the lobby, and I could tell that the night auditor hadn't arrived yet," Charlie said. "Then I walked over to the dining room doors, opened them, and saw that no one was in there. But two chairs were pulled out, and there were two glasses on a table. The next night I questioned the cocktail waitress, and she insisted that she had cleaned everything up and left the room in order. I'll always wonder whether the two figures I saw were Bill and Percie Knowles."

Charlie also found unexpected disarray in the kitchen one night after all the staff had gone home. On his first round everything was in order, but the next time he checked the area he found knives, dishes, and a variety of other utensils scattered across the cooks' table.

More than a few employees of Chico Hot Springs have reported hearing the clattering and crashing of pots and pans from the kitchen when they knew no one was there. About three weeks after he followed the ghost of Percie into room 349, Larry Bohne was tending the lobby fireplace at 3:00 A.M. and wishing he had someone to talk with.

"There were no guests in the hotel, so I was the only person on the premises," he recalled. "Even the night auditor wasn't due in for another hour and a half. But suddenly, from the kitchen area, I heard the clanging and rattling of dishes and pots and pans, as if someone were busily cooking or cleaning up.

"I knew I was supposed to be alone, so I went to investigate," Larry said. "But just as I approached the kitchen from the dining room the sounds stopped, as if someone had suddenly switched them off. I entered the kitchen, which was still dark, and when I turned on the lights, everything appeared to be in its place—nothing was out of the ordinary in any way. Immediately, I checked the exit to the outside courtyard and the door to housekeeping. Both were just as I had found them on earlier rounds, tightly secured. The only other way to enter the kitchen was from the dining room door through which I had gone myself.

"As I left the kitchen, I turned off the lights. At the same time, the telephone began to ring. Rather than go all the way back to the office, I switched on the lights again and answered the phone in the kitchen. But instead of hearing a voice on the other end of the line, I heard what I can only describe as an electrical hum, totally different from the sound of a dial tone. I hung up the phone and then picked it up to listen. This time I heard only a normal dial tone.

"I turned off the lights once again and started walking back to the office," Larry continued. "I had gotten as far as the dining room when loud music started blaring out of the kitchen.

"This time I just knew that a trickster was at work, so I sneaked back again and shone my flashlight into the room. It was completely empty, but I noticed that the music was coming from the employees' radio—though the power switch was in the off position!

"I flipped the switch on and off several times, but I couldn't get the music to stop or the volume to decrease," Larry explained. "The noise stopped only when I pulled the plug from the socket. And when I plugged the cord back in to test the radio, everything worked normally.

"Maybe what happened with the telephone and the radio could be attributed to some kind of electrical glitch," he admitted, "but this episode left me very unsettled. And I've never been able to explain away the sound of the clattering dishes when, obviously, no one was present."

During this same winter, Larry's twenty-year-old son Mike also became a security guard at Chico Hot Springs, and his initiation into "the Percie Club" was just as uncanny as his father's had been. "If Mike said something happened to him, it did," Larry insisted. "He's not one to let his imagination run wild, and the jobs he's had couldn't be done by a person who panics easily. At sixteen, for example, he was the youngest state-certified ambulance technician ever in Montana, and he's also served with search and rescue units, earning the rank of major with the U.S. Air Force Civil Air Patrol. It's also interesting to note that Mike had never heard about my experiences with Percie until after he had tangled with her himself."

Before the young man's first night of duty in the hotel, his senior partner gave him a copy of Earl Murray's *Ghosts of the Old West*. But even levelheaded Mike doubted the wisdom of reading the chapter about the Hot Springs phantom while he was alone on his first evening watch.

"But, naturally, common sense soon gave way to curiosity," Mike admitted, "so I went ahead and read it, and for the rest of that night all the creaks, cracks, and other noises kept my nerves on edge. But I didn't actually encounter Percie Knowles's ghost itself until I'd been working there three weeks, just long enough so that I no longer grew apprehensive at every little sound.

"At about three o'clock on one bitterly cold January morning, I was

THE LONELY LADY AND OTHER GHOSTS OF CHICO HOT SPRINGS

stoking the main fire and completing some paperwork after having made several rounds of the complex," he said. "Only one room on the main floor of the hotel was occupied; a few more had been rented out to guests in the lower lodge about three hundred yards from the main building. The night auditor had not yet arrived.

"I took a break and made my way through the dining room toward the restrooms in the rear," Mike continued. "As I approached the small lounge at the end of the dining room, I noticed that the tables and chairs were arranged so that there was a clear straight aisle to the restrooms. This seemed a little odd because the furniture was usually set up in such a way that you had to take a twisted path around it to get to the bathrooms.

"I also noticed that the dining room and lounge area felt unusually cold as I walked through it, and it felt just as chilly when I returned from the restroom. It's highly unusual for the area near the kitchen to be anything but cozy and warm because it usually retains the heat from the day's cooking. It also struck me as odd that several chairs were now blocking the clear path I had taken on the way into the men's room. I actually had to move them before I could get through the area and return to my office. I thought that the night auditor must have arrived early and moved the chairs for some reason.

"When I got back to the office I expected to see her, but no one was there," Mike said. "An uneasy feeling crept up my spine. To settle my nerves, I decided to take a walk around the outside of the main lodge, and as I strolled past the parking space reserved for the night auditor I saw that it was still empty.

"The air was so cold that my nose felt numb so I went back to the hotel lobby. I stoked the fire and returned to my paperwork. Soon afterward, Edie (the night auditor) arrived, booted up the computers, and went back to the kitchen to fix herself a cup of coffee. When she returned, she commented on the unusual chill coming from the kitchen, and we both attributed it to the fact that it was so cold outside.

"Edie and I were engrossed in our paperwork when we were suddenly interrupted by the sounds of dishes clinking," Mike said. "We looked up and joked that Percie must be busy at work because the kitchen crew wasn't expected for another hour. The noises continued for so long that curiosity got the best of me. As I made my way back to the kitchen, it seemed peculiar that even though I was approaching nearer to the clattering, it didn't sound any louder to me. When I was about twenty feet from the kitchen, the dish-rattling stopped completely.

"I entered the kitchen and was immediately hit with a blast of air so cold that it vaporized my breath," Mike said. "There was not much light, but as I peered across the room I could plainly see a woman with her back to me. Time seemed to come to a stop, and I felt an eerie sense of calm.

"The woman gave no sign that she noticed me," Mike continued. "She remained standing still without changing position, and I noticed that her hair was piled on top of her head. She was wearing a long dress and, as I continued to stare at her, I noticed that her hem was about six inches from the ground and nothing was visible between it and the floor.

"I felt dizzy. I was afraid to stay but more afraid to move, so I stood frozen just inside the kitchen door. Suddenly, for no apparent reason, the woman moved forward with a motion that was unlike walking. She went out a door, and I know I saw it close behind her; she was gone and the chill that had been in the room dispersed instantly.

"The door she exited from is padlocked from the outside, and there is no way to unlock it from the inside," Mike explained. "I had checked that door several times on my rounds that evening, and I knew that I had the only key to the lock except for the one that general manager Tim Barnes always keeps with him. On that night, Tim and the other set of keys were two hundred miles away in Billings, where he was attending a conference. I checked again to see if I could open the door from inside the kitchen, but it wouldn't budge."

In addition to seeing Percie's apparition and hearing her bang pots and pans around in a very chilly kitchen, the employees of Chico Hot Springs also report a variety of other phenomena apparently related to her. Security guard Charlie Wells was in the lobby one night when he heard the mysterious sound of a woman moaning. He looked for the source of the noise for at least forty-five minutes but was never able to track it down. Housekeepers hear doors slamming on the third floor when they know they're supposed to be alone on that level, and they often feel an unseen presence in the rooms there. And no matter where they place the chair that Larry Bohne saw rocking in room 349, it reputedly always returns to a certain spot facing the window. A bible in the attic is said to remain mysteriously free of dust and is always open to the same page in the Psalms, even after employees have purposely left it open elsewhere. At different times, a feather and a handkerchief have been placed on the open pages, and those who checked later found no trace of the feather and no footprints on the floor of the dusty attic. The handkerchief was found later in the saloon.

The Arts' daughter Andy believes in the ghost, but she distrusts the legend about the bible because so many people now have access to the keys to the attic. But no one has been able to explain a tray of candles that apparently lighted themselves in the kitchen, or a single candle that was found burning again after Charlie Wells knew he had extinguished it.

Charlie says that even animals occasionally sense something awry at Chico. He recalls the time that a "Heinz 57" breed of dog was so afraid to walk down a hallway that he fell, shaking with fear and wetting the carpet, when his owner demanded that he come to him.

"The Knowleses are supposedly buried just up the road from the hotel," Charlie explained, laughing. "And the security guard who helped break me in said that there's a big gopher hole in Percie's grave and that's how she got out."

In addition to giving the employees of the lodge an occasional scare, Percie apparently enjoys playing tricks on them, too. Her specialty is making things disappear—especially when they're needed the most.

"In the summer of 1991 we lost a rooming list for a group that was coming in," explained Lindy Moore. "We were all working with it out on the front desk and all of a sudden it was gone. We turned this place upside down looking for it, but we never found it. The group came and went and about a week after they had gone I walked into the office—and the list we'd been searching for was lying right out on the desk.

"On another occasion, I was the only person in the room and I set down a file to answer the phone," she continued. "When I tried to find the file again it was nowhere to be seen. But when I was getting ready to drive back home after work that day, guess what I found on the seat of my car? The file looked just as if it were supposed to be there. Things are always disappearing and reappearing in very strange places."

Percie has pulled so many pranks on the hotel staff that Edie Mundell thinks her spirit might have regressed to the time when she was twelve years old. "When I saw the ghost, I had the feeling that she was a young girl," the night auditor explained. "Maybe Percie was happiest at that time of her life and that's why I perceived her as being so young. And she certainly acts like a kid."

Edie explained that Percie is especially attracted to coins. "Once I was counting my money and I came up a nickel short," she said. "I searched for it for quite a while and then I gave up because it just wasn't there.

A couple of hours later, when I'd forgotten all about it, I found the nickel way out on the front counter. I hadn't been anywhere near that area, and I can't imagine why anyone would leave a lone nickel there."

On another occasion, Edie dropped a coin on the floor, saw where it landed, but decided to wait until she finished counting to pick it up. When she finally reached down to retrieve it, it was no longer there. Instead, it had traveled to the table where security guard Charlie Wells made out his evening reports. Charlie vouches for Edie's story and swears that he didn't take the coin himself.

Most of the strange incidents at Chico are believed to be caused by Percie, and most of the apparitions seem to be of her. But several employees have seen what they thought were male ghosts or at least spooks of undetermined gender. Many of these sightings have occurred in the area above the bar called the annex, where many employees live. Maintenance man Bob Oppelt was living in the annex in the winter of 1989, and his story is one of the most frightening of all.

"I had gone to bed and was just about to fall asleep," he recalled. "It was fairly dark but a little light from outside was coming in through the window. Suddenly, a tall figure appeared in the corner of my room. It hovered off of the ground, extending almost to the ceiling.

"I couldn't believe what I was seeing, so I closed my eyes, thinking whatever it was would go away," Bob said. "But when I opened them and dared to look again, the awful thing was still there, hovering just below the high ceiling of the room. And, even worse, it began moving, waving away from the wall and down toward me, then back again. No individual parts of its body moved; it just moved all together in this peculiar waving motion.

"I couldn't see too clearly, but the figure looked like that of a very tall man wearing something like an overcoat," Bob explained. "I could make out the definite outline of a beard and the facial features, too. My hair was standing on end and I'll never forget the eerie feeling in the air, almost like electricity. The apparition didn't reach out for me but it kept waving down toward me. Finally, after four or five motions away from the wall and back again, the ghost came right down next to me as I lay in bed.

"I tried to scream, but my throat was paralyzed," Bob said. "I remember rolling out of bed and crawling out into the hallway on my hands and knees. For quite a while I couldn't bear to go back into my room; after I finally did, I lay in bed with the light on for a long time.

"At first I didn't tell anybody about what had happened because I was afraid people would think I was crazy. I told my story only after

I found out that my brother had had a similar experience two weeks later in his room at the other end of the hall.

"His girlfriend had just come out of his room and he was lying on the bed with the light out saying his prayers," Bob said. "Suddenly, he felt something pressing on his chest, and then whatever it was started shaking him. His bed was right against the wall, making it difficult for him to get away. Then this thing started bouncing him off the wall so loudly that the guy living in the room next door could hear it. Eventually the presence went away and left my brother alone.

"I don't know if the form I saw in my room was the same thing that visited my brother," Bob said. "But I know that neither my brother nor I will ever forget what happened to us."

Andy Art was living in a small cabin across the road from the hotel when she, too, experienced an unwelcome nocturnal visitor. "I usually sleep on my side," she began, "and one night I felt something tap me on the waist. I remember flipping over, startled, and feeling that someone was in the room with me. Then I saw a hazy shape nearby. The head and shoulders were very distinct, but the rest of the body seemed to be flowing like a shapeless nightgown.

"I lay there looking at the thing beside my bed. It didn't move; it stayed in place and I sensed that it was looking at me, although I couldn't make out eyes or any other facial features," Andy recalled. "I sat up and wondered if I were still dreaming. I tried to adjust my eyes, thinking the form would disappear, but it was still there. It must have remained in my room for about ten minutes. I was terrified, but I didn't know what to do, so I just sat on the edge of my bed and looked at it. It didn't threaten me in any way and eventually it just floated away and faded from view.

"This happened in the late seventies, when I was about seventeen," Andy said. "I've always considered myself to be somewhat psychic because I often know who's calling me before I answer the phone. But that was the first time I had ever seen a ghost.

Another encounter with a vague hazy entity occurred when Andy was living on the third floor of the hotel. "I was staying at the far end, opposite the attic entrance," she explained, "and I remember getting up one night to go to the bathroom. I was walking down the hall when I looked up to see this same kind of misty cloudy form. Again, the shape of the head and shoulders was fairly distinct and everything below them just seemed to flow away to nothing. The figure was walking toward me and I was very startled. But this time it moved away and disappeared without coming close to me. I don't know if it went into a wall or what, but suddenly it wasn't there any longer. I remember having a hard time getting back to sleep after that."

Andy believes that many manifestations may be attributable to the fact that the hotel was a hospital for so many years. "I'm sure that a lot of people have come in and out of the world at Chico Hot Springs, so many spirits may reside here," she said. "I've seen phantoms two or three times in the lounge behind the dining room, and that area was at one time part of the hospital. One night, my boyfriend was in the bathroom and I was in the kitchen and, simultaneously, we both felt a presence with us. At first we each thought the other had come in to play a trick, but then we realized that that wasn't true."

Andy believes that the spirits may also be attracted to the furniture in the dining room. "There's a good chance that some of it may actually have belonged to Bill and Percie Knowles," she explained. "Lots of it dates back at least to the 1920s or 1930s, and most of the owners previous to my parents didn't put much money into new pieces, at least as far as I know."

Andy also wonders if an odd discovery made behind the hotel has anything to do with the psychic phenomena. When the Arts moved to Chico Hot Springs, they had to dig a new septic line. "Way down deep we found some very strange things," Andy said. "There were gold fillings with a piece of tooth still attached, a pair of men's beat-up shoes, and, as I recall, some eyeglasses. It made you wonder if someone had died down there, except that there were no bones or other clothing. There are many strange stories at Chico about a Chinese gardener who disappeared. Who knows if these were his things or someone else's? Finding these long-buried objects gave us a very strange feeling, almost as if we didn't want to disturb them. We felt somehow that they were supposed to be there."

Regardless of who besides Percie Knowles the other ghostly inhabitants of Chico might be, the employees agree that the paranormal activities are most common in winter and often in the dead of night, when everything is quiet and the hotel is much less busy. It is probably also significant that so many of the stories involve an intense feeling of cold and only partial materialization of spirits—from hazy indistinct figures with no discernible features to those who are so solidly formed that they look like flesh-and-blood creatures, except that they might be missing hands, or feet, or everything below the knees.

Both the coldness and the misty incomplete formation of specters may be understood more easily if we think of ghosts as manifestations of energy. The chill that so often accompanies the sighting of apparitions or other kinds of psychic phenomena may be explained by the theory that when spirits return to the earthly plane of existence they require a lot of energy to make themselves seen or heard. They may draw some of this energy from the physical environment. Heat is a form of energy, so when the ghost takes energy from its surroundings the air is apt to feel cold. As soon as the spook vanishes, however, so does the chill. Likewise, the hazy or partial materialization of spirits might be more easily understood if we liken ghosts to television signals, which are broadcast through the air to be picked up by receivers. Under conditions and circumstances not yet understood, ghosts, like TV signals, may sometimes "come in" loud and clear, while at other times their "reception" is faulty or incomplete. At these times, we might not see them at all, or they may appear misty, transparent, or even lacking crucial body parts. But if we accept the idea that any kind of manifestation requires tremendous amounts of energy, we shouldn't be surprised to find that sometimes our ghosts just aren't "all there."

Sometimes, in fact, a ghost may not look like a person at all. According to Earl Murray's *Ghosts of the Old West*, a group of teenagers and young adults were having a New Year's Eve party at Chico, and they were jumping from a roof into the hot pool. Suddenly a mysterious white light began moving along the roofline. The party-goers interpreted the light as a warning that they should get down; indeed, serious accidents had occurred previously when young people played on the roof.

There's no guarantee, of course, that anyone visiting Chico Hot Springs Lodge and Ranch will have a paranormal experience—ghosts may abound at this lovely resort, but they don't perform on demand. In fact, guests at Chico are usually so busy enjoying the pleasures of *this* world—scrumptious food, relaxing hot pools, and towering snowcapped peaks—that they have little time left to think about the next one. But if you really want to have an unearthly encounter, come to Chico Hot Springs in the dead of winter and stroll on the third floor of the hotel around three o'clock in the morning. If you catch a whiff of lilac or jasmine near room 349, put your ear to the door and listen. You might hear the sounds of the rocking chair swaying back and forth, back and forth, as a lonely lady stares from her window into the blackness of night.

Index